AF553896

Common Errors in English

COMMON ERRORS IN ENGLISH

Grenville Kleiser

A.P.H. PUBLISHING CORPORATION
ANSARI ROAD, DARYA GANJ
NEW DELHI-110 002

Published by
S.B. Nangia
A P H Publishing Corporation
4435-36/7, Ansari Road, Darya Ganj
New Delhi-110 002
Ph. : 23274050
Email : aphbooks@gmail.com

2025

Rs. 1495/-

Typesetting at
Paragon Computers
New Delhi-110 059

Printed at
Balaji Offset
Navin Shahdara, Delhi-32

PREFACE

Grammar is more than just a set of rules. It is the ever-evolving structure of our language, a field which merits study, invites analysis and promises fascination. Most commonly occurring errors are being discussed in this book:

— Missing comma after introduction phrases
— Vague pronoun reference
— Missing comma in compound sentence
— Wrong Word
— No comma in Non-Restrictive Relative Clause
— Wrong/Missing Inflected Ends
— Wrong/Missing Preposition
— Comma splice
— Possessive apostrophe error
— Tense shift
— Unnecessary shift in person
— Sentence fragment
— Wrong tense or verb form
— Subject-verb agreement
— Missing comma in a series
— Pronoun agreement error
— Unnecessary commas with restrictive clause
— Run on, fused sentence
— Dangering misplaced modified
— Its/It's Error
— Redundancy means repitition

So finally this book is very useful to students who can keep these errors in mind and learn better English.

Grenville Kleiser

CONTENTS

CHAPTER 1

A Brief Introduction

Grammar is more than just a set of rules. It is the ever-evolving structure of our language, a field which merits study, invites analysis, and promises fascination.

Don't believe us? Didn't think you would.

The fact is that grammar can be pretty dull: no one likes rules, and memorizing rules is far worse than applying them. However, as I've said, grammar is more than this: it is an understanding of how language works, of how meaning is made, and of how it is broken.

MOST COMMONLY OCCURRING ERRORS

Below is an overview of these errors, listed according to the frequency with which they occur.

1. Missing comma after introductory phrases

For example: After the devastation of the siege of Leningrad the Soviets were left with the task of rebuilding their population as well as their city. (A comma should be placed after "Leningrad.")

2. Vague pronoun reference

For example: The boy and his father knew that he was in trouble. (Who is in trouble? The boy? His Father? Some other person?)

3. Missing comma in compound sentence

For example: Wordsworth spent a good deal of time in the Lake District with his sister Dorothy and the two of them were rarely apart. (Comma should be placed before the "and.")

4. Wrong word

This speaks for itself.

5. No comma in nonrestrictive relative clauses

Here you need to distinguish between a restrictive relative clause and a nonrestrictive relative clause. Consider the sentence, "My brother in the red shirt likes ice cream." If you have TWO brothers, then the information about the shirt is restrictive, in that it is necessary to defining WHICH brother likes ice cream. Restrictive clauses, because they are essential to identifying the noun, use no commas. However, if you have ONE brother, then the information about the shirt is not necessary to identifying your brother. It is NON-RESTRICTIVE and, therefore, requires commas: "My brother, in the red shirt, likes ice cream."

6. Wrong/missing inflected ends

"Inflected ends" refers to a category of grammatical errors that you might know individually by other names — subject-verb agreement, who/whom confusion, and so on. The term "Inflected endings" refers to something you already understand: adding a letter or syllable to the end of a word changes its grammatical function in the sentence. For example, adding "ed" to a verb shifts that verb from present to past tense. Adding an "s" to a noun makes that noun plural. A common mistake involving wrong or missing inflected ends is in the usage of **who/whom**. "Who" is a pronoun with a subjective case; "whom" is a pronoun with an objective case. We say "Who is the speaker of the day?" because "who" in this case refers to the **subject** of the sentence. But we say, "To whom am I speaking?" because, here, the pronoun is an object of the preposition "to."

7. Wrong/missing proposition

Occasionally prepositions will throw you. Consider, for example which is better "different from," or "different than?" Though both are used widely, "different from" is considered grammatically correct. The same debate surrounds the words "toward" and "towards." Though both are used, "toward" is preferred in writing. When in doubt, check a handbook.

8. Comma splice

A comma splice occurs when two independent clauses are joined only with a comma. For example: "Picasso was profoundly affected by the war in Spain, it led to the painting of great masterpieces like *Guernica*." A comma splice also occurs when a comma is used to divide a subject from its verb. For example: The young Picasso felt stifled in art school in Spain, and wanted to leave." (The subject "Picasso" is separated from one of its verbs "wanted." There should be no comma in this sentence, unless you are playing with grammatical correctness for the sake of emphasis - a dangerous sport for unconfident or inexperienced writers.)

9. Possessive apostrophe error

Sometimes apostrophes are incorrectly left out; other times, they are incorrectly put in (her's, their's, etc.)

10. Tense shift

Be careful to stay in a consistent tense. Too often students move from past to present tense without good reason. The reader will find this annoying.

11. Unnecessary shift in person

Don't shift from "I" to "we" or from "one" to "you" unless you have a rationale for doing so.

12. Sentence fragment

Silly things, to be avoided. Unless, like here, you are using them to achieve a certain effect. Remember sentences traditionally have both subjects and verbs. Don't violate this convention carelessly.

13. Wrong tense or verb form

Though students generally understand how to build tenses, sometimes they use the wrong tense, saying, for example, "In the evenings, I like to lay on the couch and watch TV "Lay" in this instance is the past tense of the verb, "to lie." The sentence should read: "in the evenings, I like to lie on the couch and watch TV." (Please note that "to lay" is a separate verb meaning "to place in a certain position.")

14. Subject-verb agreement

This gets tricky when you are using collective nouns or pronouns and you think of them as plural nouns: The committee wants [not want] a resolution to the problem." Mistakes like this also occur when your verb is far from your subject. For example, "The media, who has all the power in this nation and *abuses* it consistently, *uses* its influence for ill more often than good." (Note that media is an "it," not a "they." The verbs are chosen accordingly.)

15. Missing comma in a series

Whenever you list things, use a comma. You'll find a difference of opinion as to whether the next-to-last noun (the noun before the "and") requires a comma. ("Apples, oranges, pears, and bananas...") Our advice is to use the comma because sometimes your list will include pairs of things: "For Christmas she wanted books and tapes, peace and love, and for all the world to be happy." If you are in the habit of using a comma before the "and," you'll avoid confusion in sentences like this one.

16. Pronoun agreement error

Many students have a problem with pronoun agreement. They will write a sentence like "Everyone is entitled to their opinion." The problem is, "everyone" is a singular pronoun. You will have to use "his" or "her."

17. Unnecessary commas with restrictive clauses

See the explanation for number five, above.

18. Run-on, fused sentence

Run-on sentences are sentences that run on forever, they are sentences that ought to have been two or even three sentences but the writer didn't stop to sort them out, leaving the reader feeling exhausted by the sentence's end which is too long in coming *Fused sentences* occur when two independent clauses are put together without a comma, semi-colon, or conjunction. For example: "Researchers investigated several possible vaccines for the virus then they settled on one"

19. Dangling; misplaced modifier

Modifiers are any adjectives, adverbs, phrases, or clauses that a writer uses to elaborate on something. Modifiers, when used wisely, enhance your writing. But if they are not well-considered - or if they are put in the wrong places in your sentences — the results can be less than eloquent. Consider, for example, this sentence: "The professor wrote a paper on sexual harassment in his office." is the sexual harassment going on in the professor's office? Or is his office the place where the professor is writing? One hopes that the latter is true. If it is, then the original sentence contains a **misplaced modifier** and should be re-written accordingly: "In his office, the professor wrote a paper on sexual harassment." Always put your modifiers next to the nouns they modify.

Dangling modifiers are a different kind of problem. They intend to modify something that isn't in the sentence. Consider this: "As a young girl, my father baked bread and gardened." The writer means to say, "When I was a young girl, my father baked bread and gardened." The modifying phrase "as a young girl" refers to some noun not in the sentence, it is, therefore, a dangling modifier. Other dangling modifiers are more difficult to spot, however. Consider this sentence: "Walking through the woods, my heart ached." Is it your heart that is walking through the woods? It is more accurate (and more grammatical) to say, "Walking through the woods, I felt an ache in my heart." Here you avoid the dangling modifier.

20. Its/it's error

"Its" is a possessive pronoun. "It's" is a contraction for "it is."

CHAPTER 2

More Errors

What was said	What was meant
abolishment	abolition
acrosst	across
aerobic numbers	Arabic numbers
affidavid	affidavit
afterall	after all
all goes well	augurs well
all of the sudden	all of a sudden
alphabeticalize	alphabetize
altercations	alterations
alterior	ulterior
anachronism	acronym
anticlimatic	antidimactic
anchors away	anchors aweigh
arm's way	harm's way
artical	article
ashfault	asphalt

What was said	What was meant
assumably	presumably
baited breath	bated breath
based around	based on
beckon call	beck and call
bids well	bids fair, bodes well
binded	bound
blessing in the sky	blessing in disguise
boom to the economy	boon to the economy
bonafied	bona fide
bored of	bored with
bran new	brand new
built off of	built on or upon
buttload	boatload
buttox	buttocks
by in large or enlarge	by and large
Cadillac converter	catalytic converter
card shark	cardsharp
carport tunnel	carpal tunnel
case and point	case in point
cease the day	seize the day
chalked full	chock full
cheap at half the price	cheap at twice the price

What was said	What was meant
chester drawers	chest of drawers
chicken pops	chicken pox
chomp at the bit	champ at the bit
circus sized	circumcised
dearified	clarified
cohabitate	cohabit
component	opponent
conversate	converse
conservative effort	concerted effort
copywrite	copyright
copywritten	copyrighted
coronated	crowned
coronet	cornet
cortage	cortege
a couple guys	a couple of guys
coup de gras	coup de grace
cream de mint	creme de menthe
crimp my style	cramp my style
crossified	crucified
culvert sack	cul de sac
cumberbun	cummerbund
cut to the chaff	cut to the chase

What was said	What was meant
deformation of character	defamation of character
deja vous	deja vu
Samuel R. Delaney	Samuel R. Delany
dialate	dilate
diswraught	distraught
documentated	documented
doggy dog world	dog-eat-dog world
do to	due to
down the pipe	down the pike
drownded	drowned
drownding	drowning
electorial college	electoral college
enervate	energize
escape goat	scapegoat
exasperated	exacerbated
excape	escape
exhilarator	accelerator
ex-patriot	expatriate
expecially	especially
expeculation	speculation
extracting revenge	exacting revenge
exuberant price	exorbitant price

More Errors

What was said	What was meant
fair to midland	fair to middling
far and few between	few and far between
Federal Drug Administration	Food and Drug Administration
final throws	final throes
first come, first serve	first come, first served
flustrated	frustrated
foilage	foliage
fourty	forty
foul swoop	fell swoop
genuses	genera
gleam	glean
gorilla warfare	guerilla warfare
got my dandruff up	got my dander up
harbringer	harbinger
heared	heard
heart-rendering	heart-rending
Heineken remover	Heimlich maneuver
High Iraqi	hierarchy
hobbiest	hobbyist
hold down the fort	hold the fort
howsomever	however
I seen	I saw or I" ve seen

What was said	What was meant
ice tea	iced tea
imbedded	embedded
impaling doom	impending doom
imput	input
in another words	in other words
in lieu of	in light of
in mass	en masse
in sink	inynch
in the same vane or vain	in the same vein
incredulous	incredible
insinnuendo	insinuation or innuendo
insuremountabie	insurmountable
in tact	intact
interduce	introduce
International Workers of the World	Industrial Workers of the World
intragul	integral
Issac	Isaac
ivy tower	ivory tower
jaundra	genre
just assume	just as soon
klu klux klan	ku klux klan
lacksadaisical	lackadaisical

What was said	What was meant
lambiasted, landblasted	lambasted
larnyx	larynx
laxidaisical	lackadaisical
love one and other	love one another
low and behold	lo and behold
make ends meat	make ends meet
masonary	masonry
meantime	meantime
menestrate	menstruate
meter out justice	mete out justice
misconscrew	misconstrue
mitigate against	militate against
momento	memento
muriel	mural
myocardial infraction	myocardial infarction
new leash on life	new lease on life
neck in neck	neck and neck
nip it in the butt	nip it in the bud
notary republic	notary public
odiferous	odoriferous
oject d'art	objet d'art
once and a while	once in a while

What was said	What was meant
orthoscopic	arthroscopic
overhauls	overalls
overjealous	overzealous
pacific	specific
pain-staking	painstaking
parody of virtue	paragon of virtue
part in parcel	part and parcel
pastorial	pastoral
patriarticle	patriarchal
permiscuous	promiscuous
peacemeal	piecemeal
pedastool	pedestal
periphial	peripheral
perscription	prescription
Peruvian interest	prurient interest
perverbial	proverbial
piece of mind	peace of mind
poison ivory	poison ivy
portentious	portentous
pot-bellied politics	pork-barrel politics
poultrygeist	poltergeist
predominately	predominantly

What was said	What was meant
pratfall	pitfall
pre-Madonna	prima donna
prevert	pervert
the proof is in the pudding	the proof of the pudding is in the eating
protagonist	proponent
punkin, pumkin	pumpkin
radical chick	radical chic
radioactive increase	retroactive increase
rebel rouser	rabble rouser
recreate the wheel	reinvent the wheel
repel	rappel
rot or rod iron	wrought iron
something or rather	something or other
seizure salad	Caesar salad
self of steam	self-esteem
sense of false security	false sense of security
should've went	should've gone
shutter to think	shudder to think
similiar or simular	similar
six and a half of one,	six of one,
a dozen of the other	half a dozen of the other
skiddish	skittish

What was said	What was meant
slither of cake	sliver of cake
smashed potatoes	mashed potatoes
smoking mirrors	smoke and mirrors
smothered onions	smothered with onions
somulent	somnolent
sorted past or story	sordid past or story
stain glass	stained glass
supposably or supposingly	supposedly
supremist	supremacist
thankyou	thank you
techknowledgy	technology
Theolonius Monk	Thelonious Monk
tie me over	tide me over
Tiajuana	Tijuana
took it for granite	took it for granted
tow the line	toe the line
turpentime	turpentine
tyrannical yolk	tyrannical yoke
unchartered territory	uncharted territory
unloosen	loosen
unthaw	thaw
untracked	on track or off the track

What was said	What was meant
up and adam	up and at 'em
upgraded	upbraided
Vatentimes	Valentines
verbage	verbiage
viadock	viaduct
visa versa	vice versa
vocal chords	vocal cords
voiceterous	boisterous
vunerable	vulnerable
whelp	welt
Wimbleton	Wimbledon
windshield factor	wind chill factor
witch	which
without further adieu	without further ado
world-renown	world-renowned
worse case scenario	worst-case scenario
worth its weight in salt	worth its salt or worth its weight in gold
worth wild	worthwhile

CHAPTER 3

Non-Errors

Split infinitives

For the hyper-critical, "to boldly go where no man has gone before" should be "to go boldly...." It is good to be aware that inserting one or more words between "to" and a verb is not strictly speaking an error, and is often more expressive and graceful than moving the intervening words elsewhere; but so many people are offended by split infinitives that it is better to avoid them except when the alternatives sound strained and awkward.

Ending a sentence with a preposition

A fine example of an artificial "rule" which ignores standard usage. The famous witticism usually attributed to Winston Churchill makes the point well: "This is the sort of English up with which I will not put."

Beginning a sentence with a conjunction

It offends those who wish to confine English usage in a logical straitjacket that writers often begin sentences with "and" or "but." True, one should be aware that many such sentences would be improved by becoming clauses in compound sentences; but there are many effective and traditional uses for beginning sentences thus. One example is the reply to a previous assertion in a dialogue: "But, my dear Watson, the criminal obviously wore expensive boots or he would not have taken such pains to scrape them clean." Make it a rule to consider whether your conjunction would repose more naturally within the previous sentence or would lose in useful emphasis by being demoted from its position at the head of a new sentence.

Using "between" for only two, "among" for more

The "-tween" in "between" is clearly linked to the number two; but, as the *Oxford English Dictionary* notes, "In all senses, between has, from its earliest appearance, been extended to more than two." We're talking about Anglo-Saxon here—*early*. Pedants have labored to enforce "among" when there are three or more objects under discussion, but largely in vain. Even the pickiest speaker does not naturally say, "A treaty has been negotiated among England, France, and Germany."

Over vs. more than

Some people claim that "over" cannot be used to signify "more than," as in "Over a thousand baton-twirters marched in the parade "Over," they insist, always refers to something physically higher say, the blimp hovering over the parade route. This absurd distinction ignores the role metaphor plays in language. If I write 1 on the blackboard and 10 beside it, 10 is still the "higher" number. "Over' has been used in the sense of "more than" for over a thousand years.

Forward vs. forwards

Although some style books prefer "forward" and "toward" to "forwards" and "towards," none of these forms is really incorrect, though the forms without the final S are perhaps a smidgen more formal.

Gender vs. sex

Feminists eager to remove references to sexuality from discussions of females and males not involving mating or reproduction revived an older meaning of "gender," which had come to refer in modern times chiefly to language, as a synonym for "sex" in phrases such as "Our goal is to achieve gender equality." Americans, always nervous about sex, eagerly embraced this usage, which is now standard. In some scholarly fields, "sex" is now used to label biologically determined aspects of maleness and femaleness (reproduction, etc.) while "gender" refers to their socially determined aspects (behavior, attitudes, etc.); but in ordinary speech this distinction is not always maintained. It is disingenuous to pretend that people who use "gender" in the new senses are making an error, just as it is disingenuous to maintain that "Ms." means "manuscript" (that's "MS"). Nevertheless, I must admit I was startled to discover that the tag on my new trousers describes not only their size and color, but their "gender."

Using "who" for people, "that" for animals and inanimate objects

In fact there are many instances in which the most conservative usage is to refer to a person using "that": "All the politicians that were at the party later denied even knowing the host" is actually somewhat more traditional than the more popular "politicians who." An aversion to "that" referring to human beings as somehow diminishing their humanity may be praiseworthily sensitive, but it cannot claim the authority of tradition. In some sentences, "that" is clearly preferable to "who": "She is the only person I know of that prefers whipped cream on her granola." In the following example, to exchange "that" for "who" would be absurd: "Who was it that said," A woman without a man is like a fish without a bicycle" ?"

"Since" cannot mean "because."

"Since" need not always refer to time. Since the 14th century, when it was often spelled "syn," it has also meant "seeing that" or "because."

Hopefully

This word has meant "it is to be hoped" for a very long time, and those who insist it can only mean "in a hopeful fashion" display more hopefulness than realism.

Momentarily

"The plane will be landing momentarily" says the flight attendant, and the grumpy grammarian in seat 36B thinks to himself, "So we're going to touch down for just a moment?" Everyone else thinks, "Just a moment now before we land." Back in the 1920s when this use of "momentarily" was first spreading on both sides of the Atlantic, one might have been accused of misusing the word;

but by now it's listed without comment as one of the standard definitions in most dictionaries.

Lend vs. loan

"Loan me your hat" was just as correct everywhere as "lend me your ears" until the British made "lend" the preferred verb, relegating "loan" to the thing being lent. However, as in so many cases, Americans kept the older pattern, which in its turn has influenced modern British usage so that those insisting that "loan" can only be a noun are in the minority.

Regime vs. regimen

Some people insist that "regime" should be used only in reference to governments, and that people who say they are following a dietary regime should instead use "regimen"; but "regime" has been a synonym of "regimen" for over a century, and is widely accepted in that sense.

Near miss

It is futile to protest that "near miss" should be "near collision." This expression is a condensed version of something like "a miss that came very near to being a collision" and is similar to "narrow escape." Everyone knows what is meant by it and almost everyone uses it. It should be noted that the expression can also be used in the sense of almost succeeding in striking a desired target: "His Cointreau souffle was a near miss."

"None" singular vs. plural

Some people insist that since "none" is derived from "no one" it should always be singular, "none of us is having dessert." However, in standard usage, the word is most often treated as a plural. "None of us are having dessert" will do just fine.

Scan vs. skim

Those who insist that "scan" can never be a synonym of "skim" have lost the battle. It is true that the word originally meant "to scrutinize," but it has now evolved into one of those unfortunate words with two opposite meanings: to examine closely (now rare) and to glance at quickly (much more common). It would be difficult to say which of these two meanings is more prominent in the computer-related usage, to "scan a document."

Off of

For most Americans, the natural thing to say is "Climb down off of [pronounced" offa"] that horse, Tex, with your hands in the air"; but many U.K. authorities urge that the "of should be omitted as redundant. Where British English reigns you may want to omit the "of as superfluous, but common usage in the U.S. has rendered "off of so standard as to generally pass unnoticed, though some American authorities also discourage it in formal writing. However, "off of meaning "from" in phrases like "borrow five dollars off of Clarice" is definitely nonstandard.

"Gotten" vs. "got"

In England, the old past participle "gotten" dropped out of use except in such stock phrases as "ill-gotten" and "gotten up," but in the U.S. it is still considered interchangeable with "got" as the past participle of "get."

Till vs. til

Since it looks like an abbreviation for "until," some people argue that this word should always be spelled "til" (though not all insist on the apostrophe). However, "till" has regularly occurred as a spelling of this word for over 800 years and it's actually older than "until." It is perfectly good English.

Teenage vs. teenaged

Some people object that the word should be "teenaged," but unlike the still nonstandard "ice tea" and "stain glass," "teenage" is almost universally accepted now.

Don't use "reference" to mean "cite."

Nouns are often turned into verbs in English, and "reference" in the sense "to provide references or citations" has become so widespread that it's generally acceptable, though some teachers and editors still object.

Feeling bad

"I feel bad" is standard English, as in "This t-shirt smells bad" (not "badly"). "I feel badly" is an incorrect hyper-correction by people who think they know better than the masses. People who are happy can correctly say they feel good, but if they say they feel well, we know they mean to say they're healthy.

Unquote vs. endquote

Some people get upset at the common pattern by which speakers frame a quotation by saying "quote... unquote," insisting that the latter word should logically be "endquote"; but illogical as it may be, "unquote" has been used in this way for about a century, and "endquote" is nonstandard.

Persuade vs. convince

Some people like to distinguish between these two words by insisting that you persuade people until you have convinced them; but "persuade" as a synonym for "convince" goes back at least to the 16th century. It can mean both to attempt to convince and to succeed. It is no longer common to say things like "I am persuaded that you are an illiterate fool," but even this usage is not in itself wrong.

"Preventive" is the adjective, "preventative" the noun.

I must say I like the sound of this distinction, but in fact the two are interchangeable as both nouns and adjective, though many prefer "preventive" as being shorter and simpler. "Preventative" used as an adjective dates back to the 17th century, as does "preventive" as a noun.

People should say a book is titled such-and-such rather than entitled.

No less a writer than Chaucer is cited by the Oxford English Dictionary as having used "entitled" in this sense, the very first meaning of the word listed by the OED. It may be a touch pretentious, but it's not wrong.

People are healthy; vegetables are healthful.

Logic and tradition are on the side of those who make this distinction, but I'm afraid phrases like "part of a healthy breakfast" have become so widespread that they are rarely perceived as erroneous except by the hyper-correct. On a related though slightly different subject, it is interesting to note that in English adjectives connected to sensations in the perceiver of an object or event are often transferred to the object or event itself. In the 19th century it was not uncommon to refer, for instance, to a "grateful shower of rain," and we still say "a gloomy landscape," "a cheerful sight" and "a happy coincidence."

Dinner is done; people are finished.

I pronounce this an antiquated distinction rarely observed in modern speech. Nobody really supposes the speaker is saying he or she has been roasted to a turn. In older usage people said, "I have done" to indicate they had completed an action. "I am done" is not really so very different.

Crops are raised; children are reared.

Old-fashioned writers insist that you raise crops and rear children; but in modern American English children are usually "raised."

"You've got mail" should be "you have mail."

The "have" contracted in phrases like this is merely an auxiliary verb indicating the present perfect tense, not an expression of possession. It is not a redundancy. Compare: "You've sent the mail."

It's "cut the muster," not "cut the mustard."

This etymology seems plausible at first. Its proponents often trace it to the American Civil War. We do have the analogous expression "to pass muster," which probably first suggested this alternative; but although the origins of "cut the mustard" are somewhat obscure, the latter is definitely the form used in all sorts of writing throughout the twentieth century. Common sense would suggest that a person cutting a muster is not someone being selected as fit, but someone eliminating the unfit.

It's "carrot on a stick," not "carrot or stick."

Authoritative dictionaries agree, the original expression refers to offering to reward a stubborn mule or donkey with a carrot or threatening to beat it with a stick and not to a carrot being dangled from a stick. This and other popular etymologies fit under the heading aptly called by the English "too clever by half."

"Spitting image" should be "spit and image."

According to the *Oxford English Dictionary*, the earlier form was "spitten image," which may indeed have evolved from "spit and image." it's a crude figure of speech: someone else is enough like you to have been spat out by you, made of the very stuff of your body. In the early 20th century the spelling and pronunciation gradually shifted to the less logical "spitting image," which is now standard. It's too late to go back. There is no historical basis for the claim sometimes made that the original expression was "spirit and image."

"Connoisseur" should be spelled "connaisseur."

When we borrowed this word from the French in the 18th century, it was spelled "connoisseur." Is it our fault the French later decided to shift the spelling of many OI words to the more phonetically accurate AI? Of those Francophone purists who insist we should follow their example I say, let 'em eat *bifteck.*

CHAPTER 4

SENTENCE ERRORS

Since the goal of every writer is to communicate clearly and effectively, it is important to be able to write clear, error-free sentences in essays and reports. Incomplete sentences, run on sentences, and vague wording are among the most common sentence errors in student writing (and everyone else's), which interfere with effective communication.

To help you avoid these errors and recognise and correct them in your essays, an explanation of run on sentences, comma splices, sentence fragments, and dangling modifiers, and exercises in correcting them are given below.

Run On Sentences and Comma Splices

Run on sentences and comma splices are two of the most common types of sentence error. They involve joining two complete sentences, (or independent clauses), with incorrect punctuation or no punctuation at all. A run on sentence or comma splice often seems to go on an on and causes confusion for the reader because it is actually more than one sentence.

A ***run on sentence*** occurs when two complete sentences are run together with no punctuation separating them. If the two sentences being strung together are fairly short, closely related in meaning and easily understood, they often will not be marked as an error. But if they are long and cause confusion for the reader, they are a serious problem, as they interfere with dear communication.

A ***comma splice*** is very similar to a run on sentence; it occurs when two complete sentences are joined using only a comma.

Examples:

Run on: Then chemicals such as pesticides and herbicides were used to control the pests this was effective.

Comma splice: Then chemicals such as pesticides and herbicides were used to control the pests, this was effective.

How to Correct Run On Sentences and Comma Splices

Run ons and comma splices can be corrected in several ways:

Option 1. Place a full stop at the end of the first sentence, making two separate sentences.

Correction: *Then chemicals such as pesticides and herbicides were used to control the pests. This was effective.*

Option 2. Separate the two sentences using a semicolon.

Correction: *Then chemicals such as pesticides and herbicides were used to control the pests; this was effective.*

Option 3. Link the two sentences using a comma and appropriate connecting word, called a coordinating conjunction (and, but, so, for, yet, or, nor).

Correction: *Then chemicals such as pesticides and herbicides were used to control the pests, and this was effective.*

NB Be careful when you use linking words such as therefore, however, thus, hence, moreover, and consequently (called conjunctive adverbs). If you connect two complete sentences with one of these words and a comma, you make a comma splice. Instead, place a semicolon or a full stop at the end of the first sentence or independent clause, and then begin the next one with the connecting word.

Examples:

Comma splice: *Through history human land has tried many ways to stay young, moreover, scientists of many generations have put forward various theories explaining why we age.*

Correction: *Through history human kind has tried many ways to stay young; moreover, scientists of many generations have put forward various theories explaining why we age.*

Comma splice: *For example, some nurses might feel anger or repulsion, however, patients can also be upset because they feel out of control.*

Correction: *For example, some nurses might feel anger or repulsion. However patients can also be upset because they feel out of control.*

Sentence Fragments or Incomplete Sentences

A sentence fragment is an incomplete sentence punctuated as a sentence. The fragment may be missing the subject or the verb of the sentence. Even if it has a subject and verb, if the group of words begins with a word that makes it dependent — such as *when, if, because, until, although, before, after* — it is not a complete sentence because it does not express a complete thought. This is called a dependent clause. A dependent clause needs to be attached to an independent clause to complete the meaning of the sentence.

Examples:

Fragment: *Finally, contemplating the effects of racism and whether they contribute to social cohesion or assist with division.* (This is a phrase with no subject or verb.)

Fragment: *Although Carsaniga cannot believe why this issue is so unclear to everybody and thinks that it should have been laid to rest long ago.* (This is a dependent clause; it needs to be attached to an independent clause. Alternatively, the dependent word although could be removed to make a complete sentence or independent clause.)

How to Correct Sentence Fragments

Option 1. Rewrite the sentence, supplying the missing subject or verb or both.

Correction: *Finally, society must contemplate the effects of racism and whether they contribute to social cohesion or assist with division,* (rewritten, supplying subject and predicate)

Correction: *Finally, contemplating the effects of racism and whether they contribute to social cohesion or assist with division is an essential first step in understanding this issue,* (the original phrase is the subject, predicate added)

Option 2. Join the phrase or subordinate clause to an appropriate independent clause.

Correction: *Although Carsaniga cannot believe why this issue is so unclear to everybody and thinks that it should have been laid to rest long ago, most observers believe the problem is complex,* (subordinate clause linked to an independent clause)

Option 3. If the fragment is a subordinate clause, leaving off the first word, (the subordinate conjunction), will create a complete sentence. Before doing this, be sure the sentence will make sense in the context of your writing.

Correction: *Carsaniga cannot believe why this issue is so unclear to everybody and thinks that it should have been laid to rest long ago.* (subordinate conjunction although omitted)

Dangling Modifiers:

When a sentence begins with an introductory phrase, that phrase must relate to the noun or pronoun that comes directly after it. When an introductory phrase modifies the wrong word or no word at all in the sentence it is called a *dangling modifier*. Dangling modifiers often sound vague and confusing, sometimes ridiculous.

Examples:

Dangling modifier: *Being very old and in need of repair, I paid very little money for the car.*

Dangling modifier: *Noting that there was this apparent propensity for information to jam in the bottleneck, only a small amount of information would pass through for cognitive recognition.*

How to Correct Dangling Modifiers:

Option 1. Put the noun that the phrase modifies in the dangling phrase.

Correction: Since the car was very old and in need of repair, I paid very little money for it.

Correction: *The researcher noted that because there was this apparent propensity for information to jam in the bottleneck, only a small amount of information would pass through for cognitive recognition.*

Option 2. Place the noun that the introductory phrase modifies immediately after the phrase.

Correction: *Being very old and in need of repair, the car cost very little money.*

Correction: *Noting that there was this apparent propensity for information to jam in the bottleneck, the researcher found that only a small amount of information would pass through for cognitive recognition.*

Exercises

Run On and Comma Splice Exercise

Each sentence below is a comma splice or run on sentence. Identify and correct the error in each sentence. Try using all three methods tor correcting comma splices and run ons.

1. McDonald's 12,418th outlet opened in 1991, even Moscow and Beijing have not escaped.

2. Recently scientists have made some discoveries, they have prolonged the life of some species.

3. This is caused by cross-links between peptides and hydrogen atoms furthermore due to organic chemical reactions free radicals are formed.

4. Often it is the culmination of cerebrovascular disease of many years standing in this situation a history of longstanding hypertension was a disease which contributed to the patient's Cerebral Vascular Accident.

5. There are many deficits of a CVA, the deficits I will be focusing on are Expressive and Receptive Aphasia, as

well as Hemiplegia, which are physical deficits that the patient has received as a result of a thrombotic Cerebral Vascular Accident.

6. However, the future is bright most children in Australia today are exposed to cultural difference from an early age.

7. It is the interpretation by the author of his or her imagination that we see in print, whether this is the truth or a deception is left to our interpretation.

8. Australia was then seen to be highly successful and diligent in economic growth this could have been a contribution from the high levels of immigration into the nation.

9. The financial analysts denounced the oversubscription of Qantas shares to international investors, nonetheless they avoided reporting the criterion, displaying their control and the ruling power of the media.

10. Major risk factors such as high blood cholesterol, obesity, diabetes, lack of exercise, stress, smoking and alcohol and high blood pressure may be controlled by changing our dietary and exercise habits and even our personality traits (Eysenck 1989) however it is not easy.

Sentence Fragment Exercise

Each group of words below contains a sentence fragment. Correct each sentence and try using the different methods for turning the fragments into complete sentences.

1. They may not find it easy as they will more than likely have to change a lifetime of eating habits. So too may the person who is tackling obesity.

2. Thirdly, some more discoveries on the free radical theory, next defences against oxidation and damage. Finally, the environment and the effects it has on the body and ageing.

3. Not being able to speak on the phone to her sons, or to answer questions asked by doctors and nursing staff, or being excluded from conversation.

4. An overuse of descriptive words to give the impression of power in the simple cup of tea and the ability of a "morsel of cake" to revive and regenerate a weary body.

5. Nurses must try to relieve their embarrassment. Such as giving them support by assuring them that there is nothing wrong with their intelligence.

6. On examination of the term multiculturalism, along with the history and formation of Australia's multicultural policy.

7. For example, a life threatening disease such as acute pancreatitis wherein multiple organs are affected.

8. Also the effective manager has certain personal qualities. Ability to work well under stress, being able to have and recognise new ideas, responses, and approaches.

9. Going as far as saying that the lack of tolerance and understanding of the diverse cultures throughout Australia weakens social cohesion.

10. Depending on how deeply a reader wants to analyse the use of language and characters would result in a different interpretation.

Dangling Modifier Exercise

Each sentence below contains a dangling modifier. Correct each sentence and try using both methods as you eliminate the dangling modifiers.

1. When empowered with control over their own destiny and allowed the freedom to choose, then dying with dignity could be seen as a respected right, giving back self esteem to the aged.

2. If portrayed skilfully, the reader or audience is held in suspense waiting for what will happen next.

3. After leaving school, career choices were limited for girls.

4. For example when looking at a car, information about the car is being processed in parallel.

5. Using second grade children, it was found that body build preferences, and character influenced attraction ratings, and that character had the strongest effect.

6. Being a multicultural society, the Australian calendar is peppered with ethnic festivals.

7. Whilst driving the car and listening to the radio, an accident is witnessed then focus is given to the feature of the accident.

8. Not knowing what to expect and lacking ability to cope with a particular situation, stress may affect the patient.

9. In order to be effective, the gap between cultures must be bridged by the health professional.

10. Having identified L. acidophilus as a relevant spoiling agent, the experiment has been designed to test the effects of pH as a preservative factor for the survival and control of the organism

CHAPTER 5

Correct & Incorrect Sentence

Incorrect	If oneday I am good in English, I would definitely admit it.
Correct	If someday I am good at English, I will definitely admit to it.
Incorrect	I have not 2 years meet him
Correct	I haven't met him for 2 years.
Incorrect	It is simply unimaginable on me not to fight back.
Correct	It is simply unimaginable to me not to fight back.
Incorrect	I hate my boss, I feel like kicking on his butt.
Correct	I hate my boss, I feel like kicking his butt.
Incorrect	I do not like English, so, I will go out here.
Correct	I don't like English, so I am leaving here now.
Incorrect	This is the last time I went there, as the doctor has unravel the stitches.
Correct	It was the last time that I had to go there as the doctor took out the stitches.
Incorrect	Derek, why are you come and go say nothing to us?
Correct	Derek, why did you come and go without saying anything to us?

Incorrect	I must to say that your's english is perfect. How did you learn it?
Correct	I must say that your English is perfect. How did you learn it?
Incorrect	I want to talk someone.
Correct	I want to talk to someone.
Incorrect	You are right. Just now I have leisure. Peter
Correct	You are right. I was free just now, Peter
Incorrect	I'm very sorry for yesterday, but my chief returned and I must to leave the chatroom at once.
Correct	I am sorry for my abrupt exit yesterday because my boss suddenly turned up.
Incorrect	I didn't say bye for you yesterday, please don't be angry.
Correct	I didn't say bye to you yesterday, please don't be angry.
Incorrect	John is kindness, so many people want to chat with him.
Correct	John is so kind that many people want to chat with him.
Incorrect	Had you come to Korea ? Randy
Correct	Have you ever been to Korea, Randy ?
Incorrect	Chan, are your work busy ?
Correct	Chan, do you have a busy job ?
Incorrect	I am going to a picnic.
Correct	I am going on a picnic.

Incorrect I am a bit in a hurry.

Correct I am in a bit of a hurry.

Incorrect Ah Ling, What is Hong Kong interesting.

Correct Ah Ling, What is in Hong Kong interesting.

Incorrect I'll date her out this Saturday.

Correct I'll take her out on a date this Saturday.

Incorrect My house is to ten minute of her.

Correct It is a ten minute drive from my house to hers.

Incorrect I had told you I am from China.

Correct I have told you before that I am from China.

Incorrect How do you think to learn the English ?

Correct What is your point on learning English ?

Incorrect Would you please don't ask me this question, OK ?

Correct Would you please not ask me this question, OK ?

Incorrect I'm heard music.

Correct I am listening to some music now.

Incorrect I am come from China.

Correct I am from China/I come from China.

Incorrect OK, I will see you late !

Correct OK, I will see you later!

Incorrect I wish I have....

Correct I wish I had ....

Incorrect I am going to watch the cinema tonight.

Correct I am going to a movie tonight.

Incorrect	I am difficult to learn English.
Correct	It is difficult for me to learn English.
Incorrect	I still so surprise we were born in same day.
Correct	I am so surprised that we were born on the same day.
Incorrect	Is there some topic talk about ?
Correct	Is there any topic to talk about ?
Incorrect	Give me a favor!
Correct	Please do me a favor !
Incorrect	I don't understand the meaning what you say...
Correct	I don't understand the meaning of what you said ....
Incorrect	There are not anything wrong ...
Correct	There is nothing wrong ....
Incorrect	Why not come yesterday ?
Correct	Why didn't you come yesterday ?
Incorrect	What hobby do you like ?
Correct	What is your hobby ?
Incorrect	Almost people here I never met before.
Correct	Almost all the people here are strangers to me.
Incorrect	You must be quite a character.
Correct	You are quite a character
Incorrect	In fact, Billy really owns some personality to be a VIP.
Correct	In fact, Billy really has what it takes to be a VIP.

Incorrect	Just now my connection have problem....
Correct	I just had a connection problem....
Incorrect	Joei, may be I will sleepless after I saw his pic!
Correct	Joei, I may be sleepless tonight after seeing his picture!
Incorrect	I am so boring today, please bring me fun.
Correct	I feel so bored today, please say something funny.
Incorrect	Judy: Tom sent his pic to me for long time ago.
Correct	Judy : Tom sent me his picture a long time ago.
Incorrect	You can try it more....
Correct	You can try a few times....
Incorrect	He went to abroad to further his study.
Correct	He went abroad to further his study.
Incorrect	Because that can let me more to be clear about your talk.
Correct	Because that can help me to understand what you said better.
Incorrect	Do you live there from the day your born.
Correct	Have you lived there since birth ?
Incorrect	You are very learned.
Correct	You are very knowledgeable.
Incorrect	I am sorry, my computer have the problem.
Correct	I am sorry, there is a problem with my computer.
Incorrect	Today, I'll wash my cat.
Correct	I'll give my cat a bath today.

Incorrect	How many days left for you to quit your position ?
Correct	How many days are left before you quit your job?
Correct	How many days are left until you quit your job?
Incorrect	Well, now my connection have problem.
Correct	Well, I have some problems with my connection now.
Incorrect	I writed the sentences yours down ... Maggie.
Correct	I have written down your sentences, Maggie.
Incorrect	Did Thailand come into rain season ?
Correct	Is it the rainy season in Thailand ?
Incorrect	Well, Peter!!! You must not a material boy, that is my kind too.
Correct	Well, Peter!!! You are not a materialistic person like me.
Incorrect	I'm so much pleasing to talk with you.
Correct	I'm so pleased/happy to talk with you.
Incorrect	But I had sent it for 3 days.
Correct	But I sent it 3 days ago.
Incorrect	How is going everything ?
Correct	How is everything going ?
Incorrect	I don't know how speak it in English.
Correct	I don't know how to say it in English.
Incorrect	How many mountains exist in China ?
Correct	How many mountains are there in China ?
Incorrect	How was your sleeping yesterday ? Judy
Correct	Did you have a good sleep yesterday, Judy ?

Incorrect	You're not get used to it, I guess....
Correct	You're not used to it, I guess....
Incorrect	He is trying to look cute to make himself forgiven.
Correct	He is trying to get away with it by looking cute.
Incorrect	Chen, you are informed. Thanks for your information.
Correct	Chen, you are informative. Thanks for your information.
Incorrect	Why are you come here so often ?
Correct	Why do you come here so often ?
Incorrect	Are you born in Malaysia ?
Correct	Were you born in Malaysia ?
Incorrect	Why don't stay more time here ?
Correct	Why don't you stay a little longer ?
incorrect	He was in a hospital, and he is recently out of it.
Correct	He was discharged from the hospital recently.
Incorrect	I'm also from China, but I'm live in Phillipines now.
Correct	I'm also from China, but I'm living in the Phillipines now.
Incorrect	But chat room of teacher with this chat room are difference. Right ?
Correct	But there is difference between the teacher's chat room and this chat room, right ?
Incorrect	Betty, are you investing on stock market ?
Correct	Betty, are you investing in the stock market ?
Incorrect	Can you join me the talk ?
Correct	Can I join in the talk ?

Incorrect	We have full off and half off on Sunday.
Correct	We are given the option to work either full or half day on Sunday.
Incorrect	Kelvin, don't be so jealousy !
Correct	Kelvin, don't be so jealous !
Incorrect	The China is coming into rainy weather.
Correct	China is in rainy season now.
Incorrect	All these three cities are similar warm as Malaysia.
Correct	All three of these cities are as warm as Malaysia.
Incorrect	What time of a day now in your country ?
Correct	What is the time now in your country ?
Incorrect	Comes to think of it, it sounds right!
Correct	Come to think of it, it does sound right!
Incorrect	Last one typhoon let person 4 hundred million damage.
Correct	The latest typhoon has cost the people 400 million damage.
Incorrect	But I 'm illiterature computer....
Correct	But I'm a computer illiterate ....
Incorrect	The farm can't also be escaped from that typhoon.
Correct	The typhoon has caused great damage on the farm.
Incorrect	I can't follow you two talk now.
Correct	I can't follow what both of you are talking about.
Incorrect	You must know she is jealous very much.
Correct	You must know that she is jealous by nature.

Incorrect	Seems nothing changed to me....
Correct	It seems that nothing has changed to me....
Incorrect	Will she come to there soon ?
Correct	She will go there soon, won't she ?
Incorrect	Today is very slow.
Correct	The connection is slow today.
Incorrect	But you know a lot about computer, isn't it ? I know nothing at all about it!
Correct	But you know a lot about computer, don't you ? I myself know nothing about it!
Incorrect	The sales of light arms is the main cause of heavy casualty in conflicting nations.
Correct	The sale of light arms to conflicting nations is the main cause of heavy casualties.
Incorrect	Why you want to know more about me? I am just a small people.
Correct	Why do you want to know more about me? I am a nobody.
Incorrect	Make sure that it is a high pay job.
Correct	Make sure that it is a high paying job.
Incorrect	I wonder if there is a comment on the certificate by GE about how good a student perform in the course?
Correct	I wonder if there is a comment on the certificate by GE about how well a student performs in the course?
Incorrect	We have lots of rain, because we're in monsoon season.
Correct	There is a lot of rain here as we are in monsoon season now.

Incorrect How much is the temperature?

Correct What is the temperature?

Incorrect Don't feel anger with me !!! I'm just kidding.

Correct Don't be mad at me !!! I'm just kidding.

Incorrect Kitty, your honey was left just now because I told him you will coming soon.

Correct Kitty, your honey has just left as I told him you would be coming soon.

Incorrect I am a Chinese and have been abroad 10 years.

Correct I am Chinese and have been in abroad for 10 years.

Incorrect OK, tell me how does he like ?

Correct OK, tell me what he looks like ?

Incorrect I think you should go to abroad find a job make your life a little bit changed.

Correct I think you should go abroad to find a job and make your life a little bit different for a change.

Incorrect Lilian is living far away with China.

Correct Lilian is living far away from China.

incorrect I am sure not even one man can control himself if he meet this kind of situation.

Correct I doubt that there is even one man who can control himself in this situation.

Incorrect Are you a saler, Aivin?

Correct Are you a salesman, Alvin?

Incorrect The team bring a lot of happy for football fan in the world but now I doubtful them.

Correct The team used to bring a lot of fun to the soccer fans in the world but I am doubtful of them now.

Incorrect Which kind of car ?

Correct What type of car ?

Incorrect I think your express will have a little difficult, but that is a lucky thing, I can understand you.

Correct I think you have difficulty in expressing your idea. Luckily, I can understand you.

Incorrect How are you this week ?

Correct How have you been this week ?

Incorrect I know you are good in computer and English.

Correct I know you are good at computers/computing and English.

Incorrect I think your qualification will surety make you open a computer or English training center.

Correct I think you can open up a computer or English training center with your qualifications.

Incorrect I am no exceptional.

Correct I am no exception.

Incorrect My telephone conversation with you for past one and half week has made me feel you as a very firm character.

Correct Having telephoned with you for one week, I think you have a very firm/strong character.

Incorrect It is easy or not get visa?

Correct Is it easy to get visa?

Incorrect	I wonder why are you keep study after graduated high school ?
Correct	I wonder why you keep studying after graduation from high school ?
Incorrect	He will be great help for you.
Correct	He will be of great help to you.
Incorrect	Am I a simple girl and has not any brains ?
Correct	Am I a naive lady who doesn't have intelligence ?
Incorrect	What sport are you interest ?
Correct	What sports are you interested in ?
Incorrect	Can you tell me when are you birthday date ?
Correct	Can you tell me when your birthday is ?
Incorrect	Should we continuous our speak in English language?
Correct	Shall we continue speaking in English ?
Incorrect	Do you like your female staff flirted you when you be a boss ?
Correct	Would you mind if your staff flirted with you if you were the boss ?
Incorrect	Where is the students come from ?
Correct	Where do the students come from ?
Incorrect	I wonder have you be teacher before ?
Correct	I wonder if you were a teacher before ?
Incorrect	How long does the news ?
Correct	How long does the news last ?

Incorrect	We better don't tell anothers.
Correct	We had better not tell others.
Incorrect	I am worry about your English level will getting worse if you talk to me only.
Correct	I am worried that your English will get worse if you only talk to me.
Incorrect	Come to here is more easy for you.
Correct	If you come here it will be easier for you.
Incorrect	Are they supported by Taliban or Iran.
Correct	Are they supported by the Taliban or Iran.
Incorrect	I was/got cancelled our date by her ?
Correct	She cancelled the date.
Incorrect	I will read it today night.
Correct	I will read it tonight.
Incorrect	What does differrent between 'seems' and' seem' ?
Correct	What is the difference between 'seems' and ' seem' ?
Incorrect	Then I was left this company found a another job.
Correct	Then I left this company and found another job.
Incorrect	I am the only one graduated from high school.
Correct	I am the only one graduating from high school.
Incorrect	She told me there is no another way
Correct	She told me there was no other way.
Incorrect	In fact I want my life had a little bit changed.
Correct	In fact I want to have some change in my life.

Incorrect	Oh, he has the same car with yours ?
Correct	Oh, he has the same car like yours ?
Incorrect	I have been many places in Beijing. I like this city so much.
Correct	I have been to many places in Beijing. I like this city very much.
Incorrect	There are many softwares available these days for various purposes.
Correct	There is a lot of software available these days for various purposes.
Incorrect	Let me check your pic again see how is your beautiful eyes looks like, ahha
Correct	Let me take a look at your pic again and see how beautiful your eyes look like, haha
Incorrect	I am living at Canada now, and working as a sales.
Correct	I am living in Canada now and working in sales. Or I am living in Canada now and working as a sales rep.
Incorrect	How do you think my idea ?
Correct	What do you think of my idea?
Incorrect	Am I complete right ?
Correct	Am I completely right?
Incorrect	Could you correct me this letter ?
Correct	Would you correct this letter for me ?
Incorrect	Thanks, I no longer need to wait for anyone else's opinion anymore.
Correct	Thanks, I no longer need to wart for anyone else's opinion

Incorrect	He has the aptitude for languages.
Correct	He has an aptitude for language.
Incorrect	I don't have a forum. And I also don't know how to make it too.
Correct	I don't have a forum. And I also don't know how to make one either.

CHAPTER 6

Correct and Incorrect Words

About

"This isn't about you." What a great rebuke! But conservatives sniff at this sort of abstract use of "about," as in "I'm all about good taste" or "successful truffle-making is about temperature control", so it's better to avoid it in very formal English.

Absorption/Absorption

Although it's "absorbed" and "absorbing" the correct spelling of the noun is "absorption."

Accede/Exceed

If you drive too fast, you exceed the speed limit. "Accede" is is a much rarer word meaning "give in," "agree."

Accept/Except

If you offer me Cadbury chocolates I will gladly accept them-except for the candied violet ones. Just remember that the "X" in "except" excludes things-they tend to stand out, be different. In contrast, just look at those two cozy "Cs" snuggling up together. Very accepting. And be careful; when typing "except" it often comes out "expect."

Access/Get Access to

"Access" is one of many nouns that's been turned into a verb in recent years. Conservatives object to phrases like "you can access your account online." Substitute "use," "reach," or "get access to" if you want to please them.

Accessory

There's an "ask" sound at the beginning of this work, though some mispronounce it as if the two "Cs" were to be sounded the same as the two "SS s."

Accidentally/Accidentally

There are quite a few words with -ally suffixes (like "incidentally") which are not to be confused with words that have "-ly" suffixed (like "independently").

Acronyms and Apostrophes

One unusual modern use of the apostrophe is in plural acronyms, like "ICBMs" "NGOs" and "CDs". Since this pattern violates the rule that apostrophes are not used before an S indicating a plural, many people object to it. It is also perfectly legitimate to write "CDs," etc. See also "50s" But the use of apostrophes with initialisms like "learn your ABC's and "mind your P's and Q's" is now so universal as to be acceptable in almost any context.

Note that "acronym" was used originally only to label pronounceable abbreviations like "NATO," but is now generally applied to all sorts of initialisms. Be aware that some people consider this extended definition of "acronym" to be an error.

Acrossed/Across

The chicken may have crossed the road, but did so by walking across it.

Actual Fact/Actually

"In actual fact" is an unnecessarily complicated way of saying "actually."

Add/Ad

"Advertisement" is abbreviated "ad," not "add."

Adapt/Adopt

You can adopt a child or a custom or a law; in all of these cases you are making the object of the adoption you own, accepting it. If you adapt something, however, you are changing it.

Administer/Minister

You can minister to someone by administering first aid. Note how the "ad" in "administer" resembles "aid" in order to remember the correct form of the latter phrase. "Minister" as a verb always requires "to" following it.

Adultry/Audltery

"Adultery" is often misspelled "adultry," as if it were something every adult should try. This spelling error is likely to get you snickered at.

The term does not refer to all sorts of illicit sex: at least one of the partners involved has to be married for the relationship to be adulterous.

Advance/Advanced

When you hear about something in advance, earlier than other people, you get advance notice or information. "Advanced" means "complex, sophisticated" and doesn't necessarily have anything to do with the revealing of secrets.

Adverse/Averse

The word "adverse" turns up most frequently in the phrase "adverse circumstances," meaning difficult circumstances, circumstances which act as an adversary; but people often confuse this word with "adverse," a much rarer word, meaning having a strong feeling against, or aversion toward.

Advice/Advice

"Advice" is the noun, "advise" the verb. When Ann Landers advises people, she gives them advice.

Adviser/Advisor

"Adviser" and "advisor" are equally fine spellings. There is no distinction between them.

Affect/Effect

There are four distinct words here. When "affect" is accented on the final syllable (a-FECT), it is a verb meaning "have an influence on": "The million-dollar donation from the industrialist did not affect my vote against the clean Air Act." A much rarer meaning is indicated when the word is accented on the first syllable (AFF-ect), meaning "emotion."

In this case the word is used mostly by psychiatrists and social scientists-people who normally know how to spell it. The real problem arises when people confuse the first spelling with the second: "effect."

This too can be two different words, The more common one is a noun: "When I left the stove on, the effect was that the house filled with smoke. When you affect a situation, you have an effect on it. The less common is a verb meaning "to create": "I'm trying to effect a change in the way we purchase widgets." No wonder people are confused. Note especially that the proper expression is not "take affect" but "take effect"—become effective. Hey, nobody ever said English was logical; just memorize it and get on with your life.

Agreeance/Agreement

When you agree with someone you are in agreement.

Ahold/Hold

In formal English you just "get hold" of something or somebody.

AIN'T

"Ain't" has a long and vital history as a substitute for "isn't," "aren't" and so on. It was originally formed from a contraction of "am not" and is still commonly used in that sense. Even though it has been universally condemned as the classic "mistake" in English, everyone uses it occasionally as part of a joking phrase or to convey a down-to earth quality. But if you always use it instead of the more "proper" contractions you're to be branded as uneducated.

All

Put this word where it belongs in the sentence. In negative statements, don't write "All the pictures didn't show her dimples" when you mean "The pictures didn't all show her dimples."

All Ready/Already

"All ready" is a phrase meaning "completely prepared," as in "As soon as I put my coat on, I'll be all ready." "Already," however, is an adverb used to describe something that has happened before a certain time, as in "What do you mean you'd rather stay home? I've already got my coat on."

Alliterate/Illiterate

Pairs of words with the same initial sound alliterate, like "wild and wooly." Those who can't read are illiterate.

Alls/All

"Alls I Know is...."may result from anticipating the "S" in "is," but the standard expression is "All I know is...."

Allude/Elude

You can allude (refer) to your daughter's membership in the honor society when boasting about her, but a criminal tries to elude (escape) captivity. There is no such word as "allude."

Allude/Refer

To allude to something is to refer to it indirectly, by suggestion. If you are being direct and unambiguous, you refer to the subject rather than alluding to it.

Allusoion/Illusion

An allusion is a reference, something you allude to: "Her allusion to flowers reminded me that Valentine's Day was coming."

In that English paper, don't write "literary illusion" when you mean "allusions." A mirage, hallucination, or a magic trick is an illusion. (Doesn't being) fooled just make you ill?)

A lot/A Lot

Perhaps this common spelling error began because there does exist in English a word spelled "allot" which is a verb meaning to apportion or grant. The correct form, with "a" and "lot" separated by a space is perhaps not often encountered in print because formal writers usually use other expressions such as "a great deal," "often," etc. If you can't remember the rule, just remind yourself that just as you wouldn't write "alittle" you shouldn't write "a lot."

Alright/All Right

The correct form of this phrase has become so rare in the popular press that many readers have probably never noticed that it is actually two words. But if you want to avoid irritating traditionalists you'd better tell them that you feel "all right" rather than "alright."

Alter/Alter

An altar is that platform at the front of a church or in a temple; to alter something is to change it.

Alterior/Ulterior

When you have a concealed reason for doing something, it's an ulterior motive.

Alternate/Alternative

Although UK authorities disapprove, in U.S. usage, "alternate" is frequently an adjective, substituted for the older "alternative"; "an alternate route." "Alternate" can also be a noun; a substitute delegate is, for instance, called an "alternate." But when you're speaking of "every other" as in " our club meets on alternate Tuesday," you can't substitute "alternative."

Altogether/All Together

"Altogether" is an adverb meaning "completely," "entirely." For example:

"When he first saw the examination questions, he was altogether baffled." All together," in contrast, is phrase meaning "in a group."

For example: "The wedding guests were gathered all together in the garden." Undressed people are said in informal speech to be "in the altogether" (perhaps a shortening of the phrase "altogether naked").

Alumnus/Alumni

We used to have "alumnus" (male singular), "alumni" (male plural), "alumna" (female singular) and "alumnae " (female plural); but the latter two are now popular only among older female graduates, with the first two terms becoming unisex. However, it is still important to distinguish between one alumnus and a stadium full of alumni. Never say, "I am an alumni" if you don't want to cast discredit on your school. Many avoid the whole problem by resorting to the informal abbreviation "alum."

Ambiguous/Ambivalent

Even though the prefix "ambi-" means "both," "ambiguous" has come to mean "unclear," "undefined," while "ambivalent" mean "torn between two opposing feelings or views." If your attitude cannot be defined into two polarized alternatives, then you're ambiguous, not ambivalent.

Ambivalent/Indifferent

If you feel pulled in two directions about some issue, you're ambivalent about it; but if you have no particular feeling about it, you're indifferent.

Amongst/Among

Although "amongst" has not dated nearly as badly as "whilst" it is still less common in standard speech than "among"

Amoral/Immoral

"Amoral" is a rather technical word meaning "unrelated to morality." When you mean to denounce someone's behavior, call it "immoral."

Amount/Number

This is a vast subject. I will try to limit the number of words I expend on it so not to use up too great an amount of space. The confusion between the two categories of words relating to amount and number is so pervasive that those of us who still distinguish between them constitute an endangered species; but if you want to avoid our ire, learn the difference. Amount words relate to quantities of things that are measured in bulk number words to things that can be counted.

In the second sentence above, it would have been improper to write "the amount of words" because words are discrete entities which can be counted, or numbered.

Here is a handy chart to distinguish the two categories of words:

amount vs. number

quantity vs. number

little vs. few

less vs. fewer

much vs. many

You can eat fewer cookies, but you drink less milk. If you eat too many cookies, people will probably think you've had too much dessert. If the thing being measured is being considered in countable units, then use number words. Even a substance which is considered in bulk can also be measured by number of units. For instance, you shouldn't drink too much wine, but you should also avoid drinking too many glasses of wine. Note that here you are counting glasses. They can be numbered.

The most common mistake of this kind is to refer to an "amount" of people instead of a "number" of people.

Just to confuse things, "more can be used either way: you can eat more cookies and drink more milk."

An Historic/A Historic

You should use "an" before a word beginning with an "H" only if the "H" is not pronounced: "An honest effort"; it's properly "a historic event" though many sophisticated speakers somehow prefer the sound of "an historic," so that version is not likely to get you into any real trouble.

Anecdote/Antidote

A humorist relates "anecdotes." Then doctor prescribes "antidotes" for children who have swallowed poison. Laughter may be the best medicine, but that's no reason to confuse these two with each other.

And Also/And, Also

"And also" is redundant; say just "and" or "also."

Angel/Angle

People who want to write about winged beings from Heaven often miscall them "angles." A triangle has three angles. The Heavenly Host is made of angels. Just remember the adjectival form: "angelic." If you pronounce it aloud you'll be reminded that the E comes before the L.

Anxious/Eager

Most people use "anxious" interchangeably with "eager," but its original meaning had to do with worrying, being full of anxiety. Perfectly correct phrases like, "anxious to pleases" obscure the nervous tension implicit in this word and lead people to say less correct things like "I', anxious for Christmas morning to come so I can open my present." Traditionalists frown on anxiety-free anxiousness. Say instead you are eager for or looking forward to a happy event.

Any

Instead of saying "he was the worst of any of the dancers," say "he was the worst of the dancers."

Anymore/Any More

In the first place, the traditional though now (uncommon) spelling is as two words: "any more" as in "We do not sell bananas any more." In the second place, it should not be used at the beginning of a sentence as a synonym for "nowadays." In certain dialects of English it is common to utter phrases like "anymore you have to grow your own if you want really ripe tomatoes," but this is guaranteed to jolt listeners who aren't used to it. Even if they can't quite figure out what's wrong, they'll feel that your speech is vaguely clunky and awkward. "Any more" always needs to be used as part of an expression of negation except in questions like "Do you have any more bananas?" Now you won't make that mistake any more, will you?

Anytime/Any Time

Though it is often compressed into a single word by analogy with "anywhere" and similar words, "any time" is traditionally a two-word phrase.

Anyways/Anyway

"Anyways" at the beginning of a sentence usually indicates that the speaker has resumed a narrative thread: "Anyways, I told Matilda that guy was a lazy bum before she ever married him." It also occurs at the end of phrases and sentences, meaning" in any case": "He wasn't all that good-looking anyways." A slightly less rustic quality can be imparted to these sentences by substituting the more formal "anyway." Neither expression is a good idea in formal written English. The two-word phrase "any way" has many legitimate uses, however: "Is there any way to prevent the impending disaster?"

Apart/A Part

Paradoxically, the one-word form implies separation while the two-word form implies union. Feuding roommates decide to live apart. Their time together may be a part of their life they will remember with some bitterness.

Appraise/Apprise

When you estimate the value of something, you appraise it. When you inform people of a situation, you apprise them of it.

Apropos/Appropriate

"Apropos," (anglicized from the French phrase "a propos") means relevant, connected with what has before; it should not be used as an all-purpose substitute for "appropriate." It would be inappropriate, for example, to say "Your tuxedo was perfectly apropos for the opera gala."

Artic/Arctic

Although some brand names have incorporated this popular error, remember that the Arctic Circle is an arc. By the way, Ralph Vaughan Williams called his suite drawn from the score of the film "Scott of the Antarctic," the "Sinfonia Antartica," but that's Italian, not English.

As Far As

Originally people used to say things like "As far as music is concerned, I especially love Baroque opera. "Recently they have begun to drop the "is concerned" part of the phrase. Perhaps this shift was influenced by confusion with a similar phrase, "as for." As for money, I don't have any," is fine; "As far as money, I don't have any," is clumsy.

As Follow/As Follows

"My birthday requests are as follows." This standard phrase doesn't change number when the items to follow grow from one to many. It's never correct to say "as follow."

As of Yet/Yet

"As of yet" is a windy and pretentious substitute for plain old English "yet" or "as yet," an unjustified extension of the pattern in sentences like "as of Friday the 27th of May."

As Per/In Accordance with

"Enclosed is the shipment of #2 toggle bolts as per you order of June 14" writes the businessman, unaware that not only is the "as' redundant, he is sounding very old-fashioned and pretentious. The meaning is "in accordance with," or "in response to the request made;" but it is better to avoid these cumbersome substitutes altogether: "Enclosed in the shipment of bolts you ordered June 14."

Asocial/Antisocial

Someone who doesn't enjoy socializing at parties might be described as either "asocial" or "antisocial"; but "asocial" is too mild a term to describe someone who commits an antisocial act like planting a bomb. "Asocial" suggests indifference to or separation from society, whereas "anti-social" more often suggests active hostility toward society.

Aspect/Respect

When used to refer to different elements of or perspectives on a thing or idea, these words are closely related, but not interchangeable. It's "in all respects," not "in all aspects." Similarly, one can say "in some respects" but not "in some aspect." One says "in this respect," not "in this aspect" One looks at all "aspects" of an issue, not at all "respects."

Assure/Ensure/Insure

To "assure" a person of something is to make him or her confident of it.

According to Associated press style, to "ensure" that something happens is to make certain that it does, and to "insure" is to issue an insurance policy. Other authorizes, however, consider "ensure" and "insure" interchangeable. To please conservatives, make the distinction.

However, it is worth noting that in older usage these spellings were not clearly distinguished.

American "life assurance" companies take the position that al policy-holders are mortal and someone will definitely collect, thus assuring heirs of some income. American companies tend to go with "insurance" for coverage of life as well as of fire, theft, etc.

Asterick/Asterisk

Some people not only spell this word without the secondS, they say it that way too. It comes from Greek asteriskos: "little star." Tisk, tisk, remember the "-isk"; "asterick" is icky.

ATM machine/ATM

"Atm" means "Automated Teller Machine," so if you say "ATM machine" you are really saying "Automated teller Machine Machine."

Atheist/Atheist

An atheist is the opposite of a theist. "Theos" is Greek for "good". Make sure the "TH" is followed immediately by an "E."

Augur/ Auger

An augur was an ancient Roman prophet, and as a verb the word means "foretell"- "their love augurs well for a successful marriage." Don't mix this word up with "auger, "a tool for boring holes. Some people mishear the phrase "augurs well" as "all goes well" and mistakenly use the instead.

Aural/Oral

"Aural" has to do with things you hear, "oral" with things you say, or relating to your mouth.

Avocation/Vocation

Your avocation is just your hobby; don't mix it up with your job: your vocation.

Awhile/Awhile

When "awhile" is spelled as a single word, it is an adverb meaning "for a time" ("stay awhile"); but when "while" is the object of a prepositional phrase, like "Lend me your monkey wrench for a while" the "while" must be separated from the "a." (But if the preposition "for" were lacking in this sentence, "awhile" could be used in this way: "Lend me your monkey wrench awhile.")

Ax/Ask

The dialectical pronunciation of "ask" as "ax" is a sure marker of a substandard education, to be avoided in formal speaking situations.

Axel/Axle

The center of a wheel is its axle. An axel is a tricky jump in figure skating named after Axel Paulsen.

Backslash/Slash

This is a slash:/. Because the top of it leans forward, it is sometimes called a "forward slash."

This is a backslash:/. Notice the way it leans back, distinguishing it from the regular slash.

Slashes are often used to indicate directories and subdirectories in computer systems such an Unix and in World Wide Web addresses. Unfortunately, many people, assuming "backslash" is some sort of technical term for the regular slash, use the term incorrectly, which risks confusing those who know enough to distinguish between the two but not enough to realize that Web addresses never contain backslashes. Newer browsers will silently correct this error, but older ones may not.

Backward/Backwards

As an adverb, either word will do: "put the shirt on backward" or "put the shirt on backwards." However, as an adjective, only "backward" will do: "a backward glance." When in doubt, use "backward."

Barb wire, bob wire/barbed wire

In some parts of the country this prickly stuff is commonly called "barb wire" or even "bob wire." When writing for a general audience, stick with the standard "barbed wire."

Bare/Bear

There are actually three words here. The simple one is the big growly creature (unless you prefer the Winnie-the-pooh type). Hardly anyone past the age of ten gets that one wrong. The problem is the other two. Stevedores bear burdens on their backs and mothers bear children. Both mean "carry" (in the case of mothers, the meaning has been extended from carrying the child during pregnancy to actually giving birth). But strippers bare their bodies—sometimes bare-naked. The confusion between this latter verb and "bear" creates many unintentionally amusing sentences; so if you want to entertain you readers while convincing them that you are a dolt, by all means mix them up. "Bear with me," the standard expression, is a request for forbearance or patience. "Bare with me" would be an invitation to undress. "Bare" has an adjectival form: "The pioneers striped the forest bare."

Basicly/Basically

There are "-ly" words and "—ally" words, and you basically just have to memorize which is which. But "basically" is very much overused and is often better avoided in favor of such expressions as "essentially," "fundamentally," or "at heart."

Bazaar/Bizarre

A "bazaar" is a market where miscellaneous goods are sold. "Bizarre," in contrast, is an adjective meaning "strange," "weird." Let all those as in "bazaar' remind you that this is a Persian word denoting traditional markets.

Beaurocracy/Bureaucracy

The French bureaucrats from whom we get this word worked at their bureaus (desks, spelled "bureaux" in French) in what came to be known as bureaucracies.

Beckon Call/Beck and Call

This is a fine example of what linguists call "popular etymology." People don't understand the origins of a word or expression and make one up based on what seems logical to them. "Beck" is just an old shortened version of "beckon." If you are at people's beck and call it means they can summon you whenever they want: either by gesture (beck) or speech (call).

Bemuse/amuse

When you bemuse someone, you confuse them, and not necessarily in an entertaining way. Don't confuse this word with "amuse."

Beside/Besides

"Besides" can mean" in addition to" as in "besides the puppy chow, spot scarfed up the filet mignon I was gong to serve for dinner." "Beside," in contrast, usually means "next to." "I sat beside Cheryl all evening, but she kept talking to Jerry instead." Using "beside" for "besides," won't usually get you in trouble; but using "besides" when you mean "next to" will.

Better

When Chuck says "I better get my research started; the paper's due tomorrow," he means "I had better," abbreviated in speech to "I" d better." The same pattern is followed for "he" d better," She" d better," and "they" d better."

Between

"Between 1939 to 1945" is obviously incorrect to most people—it should be "between 1939 and 1945"—but the error is not so obvious when it is written thus: "between 1939-1949." In this case, the "between" should be droped altogether. Also incorrect are expressions like "there were between 15 to 20 people at the party." This should read "between 15 and 20 people."

Between you and I/Between you and me

"Between you and me" is preferred in standard English. See "I/me/myself."

Beyond The Pall/Beyond The pale

In medieval Ireland, the area around Dublin was within the limit of English law, everything outside being considered as wild, dangerous territory. The boundary was marked by as fence called "the pale" (compare with "palisade"). The expression "beyond the pale" came to mean "bizarre, beyond proper limits"; but people who don't understand the phrase often alter the last word to "pail."

Bias/Biased

A person who is influenced by a bias is biased. The expression is not "they're bias," but "they're biased." Also, many people say someone is "biased toward" something or someone when they mean biased against. To have a bias toward something is to be biased in its favor.

Biweekly/Semiweekly

Technically, a biweekly meeting occurs every two week and a semiweekly one occurs twice a week; but so few people get this straight that you club is liable to disintegrate unless you avoid these words in the newsletter and stick with "every other week" or "twice weekly." The same is true of "bimonthly and "semimonthly," though "biennial" and "semi-annual" are less of ten confused with each other.

Blatant

The classic meaning of "blatant" is "noisily conspicuous," but it has long been extended to any objectionable obviousness. A person engaging in blatant behavior is usually behaving in a highly objectionable manner, being brazen. Unfortunately, many people nowadays think that "blatant" simply means "obvious" and use it in a positive sense, as in "Kim wrote a blatantly brilliant paper." Use "blatant" or "blatantly" only when you think the people you are talking about should be ashamed of themselves.

Bonafied/Bona Fide

"Bona fide" is a latin phrase meaning "in good faith," most often used to mean "genuine" today. It is often misspelled as if it were the past tense of an imaginary verb: "Bonify."

Born Out of/Born of

Write "my love of dance was born of my viewing old Ginger Rogers-Fred Astaire movies," not "born out of." The latter expression is probably substituted because of confusion with the expression "borne out" as in "my concerns about having another office party were borne out when Mr. Peabody spilled his beer into the fax machine." The only correct (if antiquated) use "born out of" is in the phrase "born out of wedlock."

Borrow/Loan

In some dialects it is common to substitute "borrow" for "loan" or "lend," as in "borrow me that hammer of yours, will you, Jeb?" In Standard English the person providing an item can loan it; but the person receiving it borrows it.

Both/each

There are times when it is important to use "each" instead of "both." Few people will be confused if you say "I gave both of the boys a baseball glove," meaning "I gave both of the boys baseball gloves" because it is unlikely that two boys would be expected to share one glove; but you risk confusion if you say "I gave both of the boys $50." It is possible to construe this sentence as meaning that the boys shared the same $ 50 gift. "I gave each of the boys $50" is clearer.

Boughten/Bought

"Bought" is the past tense of "buy," not "boughten." "Store-bought," a colloquial expression for "not home-made," is already not formal English; but it is not improved by being turned into "store-boughten."

Bouyant/Buoyant

Buoys are buoyant. In the older pronunciation of "bwoy" as "buoy" this unusual spelling made more sense. Now that the pronunciation has shifted to "boy" we have to keep reminding ourselves that the U comes before the O.

Brand Names

Popular usage frequently converts brand names into generic ones, with the generic name falling into disuse. Few people call gelatin dessert mix anything other than "Jell-o," which helps to explain why it's hard to find Nabisco's Royal Gelatin on the grocery shelves. All facial tissues are "Kleenex" to the masses, all photocopies "Xeroxes." Such commercial fame is, however, a two-edged sword: sales may be lost as well as gained from such over-familiarity. Few people care whether their "Frisbee" is the genuine Wham-o brand original or an imitation. Some of these terms lack staying power: "Hoover" used to be synonymous with "vacuum cleaner," and the brand name was even transmuted into a verb: "to hover" (these used are still common in the UK). Most of the time this sort of thing is fairly harmless, but if you are a motel operator offering a different brand of whirlpool bath in your rooms, better not call it a "Jacuzzi."

Brang, Brung/Brought

In some dialects the past tense of "bring" is "brang" and "brung" is the past participle; but in standard English both are "brought."

Breach/Breech

Substitute a K for the Ch in "breach" to remind you that the word has to do with breakage: you can breach (break through) a dam or breach (violate the terms of) a contract. As a noun, a breach is something broken off or open, as in a breach in a military line during combat.

"Breech" however, refers to rear ends, as in "breeches" (slang spelling "britches"). Thus "breech cloth," "breech birth," or "breech-loading gun."

"Once more into the breach, dear friends," means "let's fill up the gap in the line of battle," not "let's reach into our pants again."

Breath/Breathe

When you need to breathe, you take a breath. "Breathe" is the verb, "breath" the noun.

Bring/Take

When you are viewing the movement of something from the point of arrival, use "bring": "When you come to the potluck, please bring a green salad." Viewing things from the point of departure, you should use "take": "When you go to the potluck, take a bottle of wine."

Build off of/Build on

You build "on" your earlier achievements, you don't build" off of" them.

Bumrush/Bum's Rush

A 1987 recording by the rap group public Enemy popularized the slang term "bum rush" as a verb meaning "to crash into a show hoping to see it for free," evidently by analogy with an earlier usage in which it meant "a police raid." In the hip-hop world to be "bum rushed" (also spelled as two words) has evolved a secondary meaning, to get beaten up by a group of lowlifes, or "bums". However, older people are likely to take all of these as mistakes for the traditional expression "bum's rush," as in "Give that guy the bum's rush," i.e. throw him out unceremoniously, treating him like an unwanted bum. It was traditionally the bum being rushed, whereas in the newer expressions the bums are doing the rushing.

It's good to be aware of you audience when you use slang expressions like this, to avoid baffling listeners.

Side note: Britons laugh themselves silly when they see Americans wandering around in sportswear with "B.U.M." plastered in huge letters across their chests. "Bum" means "rear end" in the U.K.

Butt Naked/Buck Naked

The standard expression is "buck naked," and the contemporary "butt naked" is an error that will get you laughed at in some circles. However, it might be just as well if the new form were to triumph. Originally a "buck" was a dandy, a pretentious, overdressed show-off of a man. Condescendingly applied in the U.S. to native Americans and black Slaves, it quickly acquired negative connotations. To the historically aware speaker, "buck naked" conjures up stereotypical images of naked "savages" or—worse—slaves laboring naked on plantations. Consider using the alternative expression "stark naked."

By/ "Bye/ Buy

These are probably confused with each other more often through haste than through actual ignorance, but "by" is the common preposition in phrases like "you should know by now." It can also serve a number of other functions, but the main point here is not to confuse "by" with the other two spellings: ""bye" is an abbreviated form of "goodbye" (preferably with an apostrophe before it to indicate the missing syllable), and "buy" is the verb meaning "purchase." "Buy" can also be a noun, as in "that was a great buy." The term for the position of a competitor who advances to the next level of a tournament without playing is a "buy." All others are "by."

Cache/Cachet

"Cache" comes from the French verb "catcher," meaning "to hide," and in English is pronounced exactly like the word "cash." But reporters speaking of a cache (hidden horde) of weapons or drugs often mispronounce it to sound like "cachet—" "ca-SHAY"—a word with a very different meaning: originally a seal affixed to a document, now a quality attributed to anything with authority or prestige. Rolex watches have cachet.

Call the Question

This is more a matter of parliamentary procedure than of correct English, but people are generally confused about what "calling the question" means. They often suppose that it means simply "let's vote!" and some even imagine that it is necessary to call for the question before a vote may be taken. You even see deferential meeting chairs pleading, "Would someone like to call for the question?"

But "calling the question" when done properly should be a rare occurrence. If debate has dragged on longer than you feel is really warranted, you can "call the question," at which time the chair has to immediately ask those assembled to vote to determine whether or not debate should be cut off or continue. The motion to call the question is itself not debatable. If two–thirds of those voting agree that the discussion should have died some time ago, they will support the call. Then, and only then, will that vote be taken on the question itself.

Potentially this parliamentary maneuver would be a great way to shut down windy speakers who insist on prolonging a discussion when a clear consensus has already been arrived at; but since so few people understand what it means, it rarely works as intended.

Chairs: When someone "calls the question," explain what the phrase means and ask if that is what's intended. Other folks: you'll get further most of the time just saying "Let's vote!"

Callous/Callused

Calling someone callous is a way of metaphorically suggesting a lack of feeling similar to that caused by calluses on the skin; but if you are speaking literally of the tough build-up on a person's hand or feet, the word you need is "callused."

Calls For/Predicts

Glendower: I can call spirits from the vastly deep.

Hotspur: why, so can I, or so can any man; But will they come when you do call for them?

Shakespeare: Henry IV, Part 1

Newspeople constantly joke that the weather service is to blame for the weather, so we should't be surprised when they tell us that the forecast "calls for rain" when what they mean is that it "predicts," rain. Remember, wherever you live, the weather is uncalled for.

Calm, Cool, and Collected

Unless you're living in an unusually tranquil commune, you wouldn't be "calm, cool, and collective." The last word in this traditional phrase is "collected," in the sense of such phrases as "let me sit down a minute and collect my thoughts." If you leave out "cool" the last word still has to be "collected."

Calvary/cavalry

"Calvary," always capitalized, is the hill on which Jesus was crucified. It means "hill of skulls." Soldiers mounted on horseback are cavalry.

Canon/Cannon

"Cannon" used to be such a rare word that there was no temptations confuse it with "cannon": a large piece of artillery. The debate over the literary cannon (a list of officially-approved works) and the popularity of Pachelbel's cannon (an imitative musical form related to the common "round") have changed all that—confusion is rampant. Just remember that the big gun is a "cannon." All the rest are "cannos."

Note that there are metaphorical uses of "cannon" for objects shaped like large guns, such as a horse's cannon bone.

Cannot/Can Not

These two spellings are largely interchangeable, but by far the most common is "cannot"; and you should probably use it except when you want to be emphatic: "No, you can not wash the dog in the Maytag."

See also "may/might."

Capital/Capitol

A "Capitol" is always a building. Cities and all other uses are spelled with an A in the last syllable. Would it help to remember that Congress with an O meets in the Capitol Building with another O?

Caramel/Carmel

Take highway 1 south from Monterey to reach the charming seaside town of carmel, of which Clint Eastwood was formerly mayor. Dissolve sugar in a little water and cook it down until the sugar turns brown to crate caramel. A nationwide chain uses the illiterate spelling "Karmelkorn (TM)," which helps to perpetuate the confusion between these two words.

Carat/Caret/Carrot/Karat

"Carrots" are those crunchy orange vegetables Bugs Bunny is so fond of, but this spelling gets misused for the less familiar words which are pronounced the same but have very different meanings. Precious stones like diamonds are weighed in carats. The same word is used to express the proportion of pure gold in an alloy, though in this usage it is sometimes spelled "karat" (hence the abbreviation "20 k gold"). A caret is a proofreader's mark showing where something needs to be inserted, shaped like a tiny pitched roof. It looks rather like a French circumflex, but is usually distinct from it on modern computer keyboards. Carets are extensively used in computer programming. Just remember, if you can't eat it, it's not a carrot.

Caring

Most people are comfortable referring to "caring parents," but speaking of a "caring environment" is jargon, not acceptable in formal English. The environment may contain caring people, but it does not itself do the caring.

Catch-22/Catch

People familiar with joseph heller's novel are irritated when they see "catch-22" used to lable any simple hitch or problem rather than this sort of circular dilemma: you can't get published until youhave an agent, and you can't get an agent until you've been published. "there's a catch" will do fine for most other situations.

CD-ROM disk/CD-ROM

"CD-Rom" stands for "compact disc, read-only memory," so adding another "disc" or "disk" is redundant. The same goes for "DVD" (from Digital Video Disc" or "Digital Versatile Disc"—there are non-video versions). Don't say "give me that DVD disk," just "give me that DVD."

Ceasar/Caesar

Did you know that German "Kaiser" is derived from the Latin "Caesar"? The Germans kept the authentic hard "K" sound of the initial letter in the Latin work. We're stuck with our illogical pronunciation, so we have to memorize the correct spelling. (The Russians messed up the pronunciation as thoroughly as the English, with their "Czar.") Thousands of menus are littered with "Caesar salads" throughout America-named after Tijuana restaurateur Caesar Cardini, not the emperor (put they both spelled their names the same way). Julius Caesar's family name was "Julius"; he made the name "Caesar" famous all by himself.

Celibate/Chaste

Believe it or not, you can be celibate without being chaste, and chaste without being celibate. A celibate person is merely unmarried, usually (but not always) because of a vow of celibacy. The traditional assumption is that such a person is not havingt sex with anyone, which leads many to confuse the word with "chaste," denoting someone who does not have illicit sex. A woman could have wild sex twice a day with her lawful husband and techinically still be chaste, though the word is more often used to imply a general abstemiousness from sex and sexuality.

You can always amuse your readers by misspelling the latter word as "chased."

Cement/Concrete

People in the building trades distinguish cement (the gray powder that comes in bags) from concrete, (the combination of cement, water, sand, and gravel which becomes hard enough in your driveway to drive your car on). In contexts where technical precision matters, it's probably better to speak of a "concrete sidewalk" rather than of a "cement sidewalk."

Center Around/Center on, Revolve Around

Two perfectly good expressions—"center on" and "revolve around" –get conflated in this nonsensical neologism. When a speaker says his address will "center around the topic of" whatever, my interest level plummets.

Center of Attraction/Center of Attention

"Center of attraction" makes perfect sense, but the standard saying is "center of attention."

Chai Tea/Chai

"Chai" is simply the word for "tea" in Hindi and several other Asian languages. The spicy, milky variety know in India as "masala chai" is called "chai" in the U.S. Since Americans likely to be attracted by the word "chai" already know it's a tea-based drink, it's both redundant and pointless to call the product "chai tea."

Chaise longue

When English speakers want to be elegant they commonly resort to French, often mangling it in the process. The entrée [acute accent over the second E], the dish served before the plat, usurped the latter's position as main dish. And how in the world did French "lingerie" (originally meaning linen goods of all sorts, later narrowed to underwear only) pronounced --roughly-- "lanzheree" come to be American "lawnzheray"? Quelle horreur! "Chaise lounge" (literally "long chair"), pronounced—roughly—"shezz lohng" with a hard G on the end became in English "shayz long." Many speakers, however, confuse French chaise with English "chase" and French lounge with English "lounge" (understandable since the article in question is a sort of couch or lounge), resulting in the mispronunciation "chase lounge." We may imagine the French as chasing each other around their lounges, but a chaise is just a chair.

Chemicals

Markets offering "organic" produce claim it has been raised "without chemicals." News stories fret about "chemicals in our water supply." This common error in usage indicates quite clearly the lamentable level of scientific literacy in our population. Everything on earth save a few stray subatomic particles and various kinds of energy (and—if you believe in it—pure spirit) is composed of chemicals. Pure water consists of the chemical dihydrogen oxide. Vitamins and minerals are chemicals. In the broadest sense, even simple elements like nitrogen can be called chemicals. Writers who use this term sloppily contribute to the obfuscation of public debate over such serious issues as pollution and malnutrition.

Chicano/Latino/Hispanic

"Chicano" means "Mexican-American," and not all the people denoted by this term like it. When speaking of people from various other Spanish-speaking countries, "Chicano" is an error for "Latino" or "Hispanic." Only "Hispanic" can include people with a Spanish as well as with a Latin American heritage; and only "Latino" could logically include protuguese-speaking Brazilians, though that is rarely done.

Chunk/Chuk

In casual conversation, you may get by with saying "Chuck (throw) me that monkey wrench, will you?" But you will mark yourself as illiterate beyond mere casualness by saying instead "Chunk me that wrench." This is a fairly common substitution in some dialects of American English.

Church

Catholics routinely refer to their church as the Church, with a capital "C." This irritates the members of other churches, but is standard usage. When "church" stands by itself (that is, not as part of a name like "First Methodist Church") capitalize it only to mean "Roman Catholic Church."

Cite/Site/Sight

You cite the author in an endnote; you visit a Web site or the site of the crime, and you sight your beloved running toward you in slow motion on the beach (a sight for sore eyes!).

Cleanup/Clean UP

"Cleanup" is usually a noun: "the cleanup of the toxic waste site will cost billions of dollars." "Clean" is a verb in the phrase "clean up": "You can go the mall after you clean up your room."

Cliché/Cliched

One often hears young people say "That movie was so cliché!" "Cliché" is a noun, meaning an overfamiliar phrase or image. A work containing clichés is clichéd.

Click/Clique

Students lamenting the division of their schools into snobbish factions often misspell "clique" as "click." In the original French, "clique" was synonymous with "claque"—an organized group of supporters at a theatrical even who tried to prompt positive audience response by clapping enthusiastically.

Close/Clothes

Because the TH in "Clothes" is seldom pronounced distinctly, it is often misspelled "close." Just remember TH in "clothing," where it is obvious. Clothes are made of cloth. Rage can also be cloths (without an E).

Coarse/Course

"Coarse" is always an adjective meaning "rough, crude." Unfortunately, this spelling is often mistakenly used for a quite different word, "course," which can be either a verb or a noun (several different meanings).

Colombia/Columbia

Although both are named after Columbus, the U.S. capital is the District of Columbia, whereas the south American country is Colombia.

Compare and Contrast

Hey kids, here's a chance to catch your English teacher in a redundancy!

To compare two things is to note their similarities and their differences. There's no need to add "and contrast."

Compare to/Compare with

These are sometimes interchangeable, but when you are stressing similarities between the items compared, the most common word is "to": "She compared his homė-made wine to toxic waste." If fou are examining both similarities and differences, use "with": The teacher compared Steve's exam with Robert's to see whether they had cheated."

Complement/Compliment

Originally these two spellings were used interchangeably, but they have come to be distinguished from each other in modern times. Most of the times the word people intend is "compliment": nice things said about someone ("She paid me the compliment of admiring the way I shined my shoes."). "Complement," much less common, has a number of meanings associated with matching or completing. Complements supplement each other, each adding something the others lack, so we can say that "Alice's love for entertaining and Mike's love for washing dishes complement each other." Remember, if you're not making nice to someone, the word is "complement."

Complementary/Complimentary

When paying someone a compliment like "I love what you've done with the kitchen!" you're being complimentary. A free bonus item is also a complimentary gift. But colors that go well with each other are complementary.

Comprised of/Composed of

Although "comprise" is used primarily to mean "to include," it is also often stretched to mean "is made up of"-- a meaning that some critics object to. The most cautious route is to avoid using "of" after any form of "comprise" and substitute "is composed of" in sentences like this: "Jimmy's paper on Marxism was composed entirely of sentences copied off the Marx Brothers Home Page."

Concensus/Consensus

You might suppose that this word had to do with taking a census of the participants in a discussion, but it but it doesn't. It is a good old Latin word that has to do with arriving at a common sense of the meeting, and the fourth letter is an "S."

Conflicted/Conflicting Feelings

Phrases like "conflicted feelings" or "I feel conflicted" are considered jargon by many, and out of place in formal writing. Use "I have conflicting feelings" instead, or write "I feel ambivalent."

Confusionism/Confucianism

This spelling error isn't exactly an English error, but it's very common among my students. Confucius is the founder of Confucianism. His name is not spelled "Confucious," and his philosophy is not called "Confusionism." When you spot the confusion in the latter term, change it quickly to "Confucianism."

Congradulations/Congratulations

I fear that all too many people are being "congradulated" for graduating from high school who don't know that this word should be spelled "congratulations." Try a search for this misspelling on your favorite Web search engine and be prepared to be astonished.

Continual/Continuous

"Continuous' refers to actions which are uninterrupted: "My upstairs neighbor played his stereo continuously from 6:00 PM to 3:30 AM." Continual actions, however, need not be uninterrupted, only repeated: "My father continually urges me to get a job."

Conversate/Converse

"Conversate" is what is called a "back-formation" based on the noun "conversation." But the verb for this sort of thing is "converse."

Core/Corps/Corpse

Apples have cores. A corps is an organization, like the peace corps. A corpse is a dead body, a carcass.

Collaborate/Corroborate

People who work together on a project "collaborate" (share their labor); people who support your testimony as a witness "corroborate" (strengthen by confirming) it.

Colons/Semicolons

Colons have a host of uses, but they moistly have in common that the colon acts to connect what precedes it with what follows. Think of the two dots of a colon as if they were stretched out to form an equal sign, so that you get cases like this: "he provided all the ingredients: sugar, flour, butter, and vanilla."

There are a few exceptions to this pattern, however. One unusual use of colons is in between the chapter and verses of a biblical citation, for instance, "Matthew 6:5" In bibliographic citation a colon separates the city from the publisher: "New York: New Directions, 1979." It also separates minutes from hours in times of day when given in figures: "8:35." It is incorrect to substitute a semicolon in any of these cases.

Think of the semicolon as erecting a little barrier with that dug-in comma under the dot; semicolons always imply separation rather that connection. A sentence made up of two distinct parts whose separation needs to be emphasized may do so with a semicolon: "Mary moved to seattle; she was sick of getting sunburned in Los Angeles." When a compound sentence contains commas within one or more of its clauses, you have to escalate to a semicolon to separate the clauses themselves: "It was a mild, deliciously warm spring day; and Mary decided to walk to the fair." The other main use of semicolons is to separate one series of items from another—a series within a series, if you will: "The issues discussed by the board of directors were many: the loud, acrimonious complaints of the stockholders; the abrupt, devastating departure of the director; and the startling, humiliating discovery that he had absconded with half the company's assets." Any time the phrases which make up a series contain commas, for whatever reason, they need to be separated by semicolons.

Many people are so terrified of making the wrong choice that they try to avoid colons and semicolons altogether, but I'm afraid this just can't be done. Formal writing requires their use, and it's necessary to learn the correct patterns.

Contrasts/Contrasts with

"With" must not be omitted in sentences like this: "Julia's enthusiasm for rugby contrasts with Cheryl's devotion to chess."

Could Care Less/Couldn't Care Less

Clinches are especially prone to scrambling because they become meaningless thorough overuse. In this case an expression which originally meant "it would be impossible for me to care less than I do because I do not care at all" is rendered senseless by being transformed into the now—common "I could care less." Think about it: if you could care less, that means you care some. The original already drips sarcasm, so it's pointless to argue that the newer version is "ironic." People who misuse this phrase are just being careless.

Could of, Should of, Would of/Could have, Should have, Would have

This is one of those errors typically made by a person more familiar with the spoken that the written from of English. A sentence like. I would have gone if anyone had given me free tickets" is normally spoken in a slurred way so the two words "would have" are not distinctly separated, but blended together into what is properly rendered "would" ve. "Seeing that "V" tips you off right away that "would" ve" is a contraction of "would have." But many people hear "would of" and that's how they write it. Wrong.

Note that "must of" is similarly an error for "must have."

Council/Counsel/Consul

The first two words are pronounced the same but have distinct meanings. An official group that deliberates, like the Council on Foreign Relations, is a "council"; all the rest are "counsels": your lawyer, advice, etc. A consul is a local representative of a foreign government.

Couple/Couple of

Instead of "she went with a couple sleazy quays before she met me," write "a couple of guys" if you are trying to sound a bit more formal. Leaving the "of" out is a casual, slangy pattern.

Credible/Credulous

"Credible" means "believable" or "trustworthy." It is also used in a more abstract sense, meaning something like "worthy": "She made a credible lyric soprano." Don't confuse "credible" with "credulous," a much rarer word which means "gullible." "He was incredulous" means "he didn't believe it" whereas "he was incredible" means "he was wonderful" (but use the latter expression only in casual speech).

Crescendo/Climax

When something is growing louder or more intense, it is going through a crescendo (from an Italian word meaning "growing"). Traditionalists object to its use when you mean "climax." A crescendo of cheers by an enthusiastic audience grows until it reaches a climax, or peak. "Crescendo" as a verb is common, but also disapproved by many authorities. Instead of "the orchestra crescendos," write "the orchestra plays a crescendo."

Criteria/Criterion

There are several words with Latin or Greek roots whose plural forms ending in a are constantly mistaken for singular ones. See, for instance, data and media. You can have one criterion or many criteria. Don't confuse them.

Critique/Criticize

A critique is a detailed evaluation of something. The formal way to request one is "give me your critique," though people often say informally "critique this"—meaning "evaluate it thoroughly." But "critique" as a verb is not synonymous with "criticize" and should not be routinely substituted for it. "Josh critiqued my backhand" means Josh evaluated your tennis technique but not necessarily that he found it lacking. "Josh criticized my backhand" means that he had a low opinion of it.

You can write criticism on a subject, but you don't criticize on something, you just criticize it.

Crucifiction/Crucifixion

One might suppose that this common misspelling was a product of skepticism were it not for the fact that it most often occurs in the writings of believers. The word should make clear that Jesus was affixed to the cross, not imply that his killing is regarded as a fiction.

Currant/Current

"Current" is an adjective having to do with the present time, and can also be a noun naming a thing that, like time, flows:

electrical current, currents of public opinion. "Currant" refers only to little fruits.

Cut and Dry/Cut and Dried

Many people mishear the standard expression meaning "set," "not open to change," as "cut and dry." Although this form is listed in the Oxford English Dictionary, it is definitely less common in sophisticated writing. The dominant modern usage is "Cut-and-dried "When used to modify a noun, it must be hyphenated: "cut-and-dried plan."

Cut And Paste/Copy and paste

Because "cut and paste" is a familiar phrase, many people say it when they mean "copy and paste" in a computer context. This can lead to disastrous results if followed literally by an inexpert person. If you mean to tell someone to duplicate something rather than move it, say "copy." And when you are moving bits of computer information from one place to another the safest sequence is often to copy the original, paste the copy elsewhere, and only them delete (cut) the original.

Damped/Dampened

When the vibration of a wheel is reduced it is damped, but when you drive through a puddle your tire is dampened. "Dampened" always has to do with wetting, if only metaphorically: "The announcement that Bob's parents were staying home after all dampened the spirits of the party-goers." The parents are being a wet blanket.

Data/Datum

There are several words with Latin or Greek roots whose plural forms ending in A are constantly mistaken for singular ones. See, for instance, "criteria" and "media." "Datum" is so rare now in English that people may assume "data" has no singular form. Many American usage communities, however, use "'data" as a singular and some have even gone so far as to invent "datum's" as a new plural. This is a case where you need to know the patterns of your context. An engineer or scientist used to writing "the data is" may well find that the editors of a journal or publishing house insist on changing this phrase to "the data are." Usage is so evenly split in this case that there is no automatic way of determining which is right; but writers addressing an international audience of non specialists would probably be safer treating "data" as plural.

Decimate/Annihilate, Slaughter, Etc.

This comes under the heading of the truly picky. Despite the fact that most dictionaries have caved in, some of us still remember that when the Romans killed one out of every ten (decem) soldiers in a rebellious group as an example to the other, they decimated them. People sensitive to the roots of words are uncomfortably reminded of that ten percent figure when they see the word used instead to mean "annihilate," "obliterate," etc. You can usually get away with using "decimate" to mean "drastically reduce in numbers," but you're taking a bigger risk when you use it to mean "utterly wipe out."

Deep-Seeded/Deep-Seated

Those who pine for the oral cultures of YOlden Days can rejoice as we enter an era where many people are unfamiliar with common expressions in print and know them only by hearsay. *The result is mistakes like "deep seeded." The expression has nothing to do with a feeling being planted deep within one, but instead refers to its being seated firmly within one's breast: "My aversion to anchovies is deep-seated." Compounding their error, most people who misuse this phrase leave the hyphen out. Tennis players may be seeded, but not feelings.

*The notion that English should be spelled as it pronounced is widespread, but history is against the reformers in most cases. Pronunciation is often a poor guide to spelling. The veneration of certain political movements for the teaching of reading through phonics is nicely caricatured by a t-shirt slogan I've seen: "Hukt awn fonix."

Defence/Defense

If you are writing for a British publication, use "defense," but the American "defense" has the advantages of greater antiquity, similarity to the words from which it was derived, and consistency with words like "defensible."

Definate/Definite

Any vowel in an unstressed position can sometimes have the sound linguists call a "schwa:" "uh." The result is that many people tend to guess when they hear this sound, but "definite" is definitely the right spelling. Also common are various misspellings of "definitely," including the bizarre "defiantly."

Defuse/Diffuse

You defuse a dangerous situation by treating it like a bomb and removing its fuse; to diffuse, in contrast, is to spread something out: "Bob's cheap cologne diffused thought the room, wrecking the wine-tasting."

Degrade/Denigrate/Downgrade

Many people use "downgrade" instead of "denigrate" to mean "defame, slander," "Downgrade" is entirely different in meaning. When something is downgraded, it is lowered in grade (usually made worse), not just considered worse. "When that president of the company fled to Rio with fifteen million dollars, its bonds were downgraded to junk bond status."

"Degrade" is much more flexible in meaning. It can mean to lower in status or rank (like "downgrade") or to corrupt or make contemptible; but it always has to do with actual reduction in value rather than mere insult, like "denigrate." Most of the time when people use "downgrade" they would be better of instead using "insult," "belittle," or "sneer at."

Deja vu

In French "deja vu" means literally "already seen" and usually refers to something excessively familiar. However the phrase, sans accent marks, was introduced into English mainly as a psychological term indicating the sensation one experiences when feeling that something has been experienced before when this is in fact not the case. If you feel strongly that you have been previously in a place where you know for a fact you have never before been, you are experiencing a sensation of deja vu. English usage is rapidly sliding back toward the French meaning, confusing listeners who expect the phrase to refer to a false sensation rather than a factual familiarity, as in "Congress is in session and talking about campaign finance reform, creating a sense of deja vu." In this relatively new sense, the phrase has the same associations as the colloquial "same old, same old" (increasingly often misspelled "sameo, sameo" by illiterates).

"It seems like it's deja vu all over again," is redundantly mangled saying usually attributed to baseball player Yogi Berra. Over the ensuing decades clever writers would allude to this blunder in their prose by repeating the phrase "deja vu all over again," assuming that their readers would catch the allusion and share a chuckle with them. Unfortunately, recently the phrase has been worn to a frazzle and become all but substituted for the original, so that not only has it become a very tired joke indeed—a whole generation has grown up thinking that Berra's malapropism is the correct form of the expression. Give it a rest, folks!

Democrat Party/Democratic Party

Certain Republican members of Congress have played the childish game in recent years of referring to the opposition as the "Democrat party," hoping to imply the Democrats are not truly democratic. They succeed only in making themselves sound ignorant, and so will you if you imitate them. The name is "Democratic party."

Depends/Depends on

In casual speech, we say "it depends who plays the best defense"; but in writing follow "depends" with "on."

Depreciate/Deprecate

To depreciate something is to actually make it worse, whereas to deprecate something is simply to speak or think of it in a manner that demonstrates your low opinion of it.

Desert/Dessert

Perhaps these two words are confused partly because "dessert" is one of the few words in English with a double "s" pronounced like "z" ("brassiere" is another). That impoverished stretch of sand called a desert can only afford one "S." In contrast, that rich gooey extra thing at the end of the meal called a dessert indulges in two of them. The word in the phrase "he got his just deserts" is confusingly pronounced just like "desserts."

Device/Devise

"Device" is a noun. A can-opener is a device. "Devise" is a verb. You can devise a plan for opening a can with a sharp rock instead. Only in law is "devise" properly used as a noun, meaning something deeded in a will.

Dialogue/Discuss

"Dialogue" as a verb in sentences like "the Math department will dialogue with the Dean about funding" is commonly used jargon in business and education settings; but abhoreed by traditionalists. Say "have a dialogue" or "discuss" instead.

Dieties/Deities

This one is always good for a laugh. The gods are deities, after the Lat in "deus," meaning "god."

Different Than/Different From/To

Americans say "scuba-diving is different from snorkeling," the British sometimes say "different to" and those who don't know any better say "different than."

Differ/Vary

"Vary" can mean "differ," but saying "our opinions vary" makes it sound as if they were changing all the time when what you really mean is "our opinions differ." Pay attention to context when choosing one of these words.

Dilemma/Difficulty

A dilemma is a difficult choice, not just any difficulty or problem. Whether to invite your son's mother to his high school graduation when your current wife hates her is a dilemma. Cleaning up after a hurricane is just a problem, though a difficult one.

Dire Straights/Dire Straits

When you are threading your way through troubles as if you were traversing a dangerously narrow passage you are in "dire straits." The expression and the band by that name are often transformed by those who don't understand then word "strait" into "dire straights."

Disburse/Disperse

You disburse money by taking it out of your purse (French "bourse") and distributing it. If you refuse to hand out any money, the eager mob of beggars before you may disperse (scatter).

Disc/Disk

"Compact disc" is spelled with a "C" because that's how its inventors decided it should be rendered; but a computer disk is spelled with a "K" (unless it's a CD-ROM, of course). The New York Times insisted for many years on the spelling "compact disk" in its editorial pages, often incongruously next to ads containing the copyrighted spelling "disc"; but now even it has given in.

Discreet/Discrete

The more common word is "discreet," meaning "prudent, circumspect"; "When arranging the party for Agnes, be sure to be discreet; we want her to be surprised." " Discrete" means "separate, distinct": "He arranged that guest list into two discrete groups: meat-eaters and vegetarians." Note how the T separates the two Es in "discrete."

Discussed/Disgust

"Discussed" is the past tense of the verb "discuss." Don't substitute for it the noun "disgust" in such sentences as "The couple's wedding plans were thoroughly discussed."

Disinterested/Uninterested

A bored person is uninterested. Do not confuse this word with the much rarer "disinterested," which means "objective, neutral".

Doctorial/Doctoral

"Doctoral" is occasionally misspelled—and often mispronounced—"doctorial."

Dolly/Handcart

A dolly is a flat platform with wheels on it, often used to make heavy objects mobile, or by an auto mechanic lying on one under a car body. Many people mistakenly use this word to designate the vertically oriented two-wheeled device with upright handles and horizontal lip. This latter device is more properly called a "handcart" or "hand truck."

Dominate/Dominant

The verb is "dominate"; the adjective is "dominant." The dominant chimpanzee tends to dominate the others.

Done/Did

The past participle of "do" is "done," so it's not "they have did what they promised not to do" but "they have done——" But without a helping verb, the word is "did." Nonstandard: "I done good on the test.

Standard: I did well on the test."

Doubt That/Doubt Whether/Doubt If

If you really doubt that something is true (suspect that it's false), use "doubt that" : "I doubt that Fred has really lost 25 pounds." If you want to express genuine uncertainty, use "whether": "I doubt whether we'll see the comet if the clouds don't clear soon." "Doubt if" can be substituted for "doubt whether," though it's considered somewhat more casual, but don't use it when you mean "doubt that."

Doubtlessly/Doubtless

Leave off the unnecessary "-ly" in "doubtless."

Dove/Dived

Although "dove" is a common form of the past tense of "dive," a few authorities consider "dived" preferable in formal writing.

Downfall/Drawback

A downfall is something that causes a person's destruction, either literal or figurative: "expensive cars Fred's downfall: he spent his entire inheritance on them and went bankrupt. " A drawback is not nearly so drastic, just a flaw or problem of some kind, and is normally applied to plans and activities, not to people: "Gloria's plan to camp on Mosquito Island had just one drawback: she had forgotten to bring her insect repellent." Also, "downfall" should not be used when the more moderate "decline" is meant; reserve it for ruin, not to designate simple deterioration.

Drank/Drunk

Many common verbs in English change form when their past tense is preceded by an auxiliary ("helping") verb: I ran, I have run." The same is true of "drink." Don't say "I've drank the beer" unless you want people to think you are drunk. An even more common error is "I drunk all the milk." It's " I've drunk the beer" and "I drank all the milk."

Drier/Dryer

A clothes dryer makes the clothes drier.

Dribble/Drivel

"Dribble" and "drivel" originally meant the same thing: drool. But the two words have become differentiated. When you mean to criticize someone else's speech as stupid or pointless, the word you want is "drivel."

Drive/Disk

A hard drive and a hard disk are much the same thing; but when it comes to removable computer media, the drive is the machinery that turns and reads the disk. Be sure not to ask for a drive when all you need is a disk.

Drug/Dragged

"Well, look what the cat drug in! Unless you are trying to render dialectical speech to convey a sense of down-home rusticity, use "dragged" as the past of "drag."

Dual/Duel

"Dual" is an adjective describing the two-ness of something—dual carburetors, for instance. A "duel" is a formal battle intended to settle a dispute.

Duck Tape/Duct Tape

A commercial firm has named its product "Duck Tape," harkening back to the original name for this adhesive tape (which was green), developed by Johnson & Johnson during World War II to waterproof ammunition cases. It is now usually called "duct tape," for its common use in connecting ventilation and other ducts (which match its current silver color).

Due to The Fact that/Beacause

Although "due to" is now a generally acceptable synonym for "because," "due to the fact that" is a clumsy and wordy substitute that should be avoided in formal writing. "Due to" is often misspelled "do to."

Dyein/Dying

If you are using dye to change your favorite t-shirt from which to blue you are dyeing it; but if you don't breathe for so long that your face turns blue, you may be dying.

E.G. / I.E.

When you mean "for example," use e.g. it is an abbreviation for the Latin phrase example gratia. When you mean "that is," use "i.e." It is an abbreviation for the Latin phrase id est. Either can be used to clarify a preceding statement, the first by example, the second by restating the idea more clearly or expanding upon it. Because these uses are so similar, the two abbreviations are easily confused. If you just stick with good old English "for example" and "that is" you won't give anyone a chance to sneer at you. If you insist on using the abbreviation, perhaps "example given" will remind you to use "e.g.," while "in effect" suggests "I.E."

Each

"Each" as a subject is always singular: think of it as equivalent to "every one." The verb whose subject it is must also be singular. Some uses, like "to keep them from fighting, each dog has been given its own bowl," cause no problem. No one is tempted to say "have been given." But when a prepositional phrase with a plural object intervenes between subject and verb, we are likely to be misled into saying things like "Each of the children have to memorize their own licker combinations." The subject is "each," not "children." The tendency to avoid specifying gender by using "their" adds to pressure toward plurality; but the correct version of this sentence is "Each of the children has to memorize his or her own locker combination." One can avoid the entire problem by pluralizing throughout: "All the children have to memorize their own licker combinations" (but see the entry on singuilar "they"). In many uses, however, "each" is not the subject, as in "We each have our own favorite flavor of ice cream" which is correct because "we" and not "each" is the subject of the verb "have."

"Each other" cannot be a subject, so the question of verb number does not arise; but the number of the possessive creates a problem for some writers. "They gazed into each other's eyes" is correct and "each others" is incorrect because "each other" is singular. Reword to "each gazed into the other's eyes" to see the logic behind this rule. "Each other" is always two distinct words separated by a space although it functions grammatically as a sort of compound word.

Earth, Moon

Soil is lower-case "earth." And in most uses even the planet itself remains humbly in lower-case letters: "peace on earth." But in astronomical contexts, the Earth comes into own with a proud initial capital, and in science fiction it drops the introductory article and becomes "earth," just like Mars and Venus. A similar pattern applies to Earth's satellite: "Shine on, harvest moon," but "from the Earth to the Moon. Because other planets also have moons, it never loses its article.

Ecology/Environment

"Ecology" is the study of living things in relationship to their environment. The word can also be used to describe the totality of such relationship; but it shouldn't be substituted for "environment" in statements like "improperly discarded lead batteries harm the ecology." It's not the relationships that are being harmed, but nature itself: the batteries are harming the environment.

Economical/Economic

Something is economical if it saves you money; but if you're talking about the effect of some measure on the world's economy, it's an economic effect.

Ecstatic

Pronounced "eck-sta-tic," not "eass-ta-tic."

Ect./Etc.

"Etc." is an abbreviation for the Latin phrase et cetera, meaning "and other." (Et means "and" in French too.) Just say "et cetera" out loud to yourself to remind yourself of the correct order of the "T" and "C. Also to be avoided is the common mispronunciation "excetera." "and is a redundancy "And etc." is a redundancy.

-Ed/-Ing

In some dialects it is common to say "my shoes need shined" instead of the standard "my shoes need shining" or "my shoes need to be shined."

-Ed/-T

You have learnt you lessons only in U.K.-influenced contries, you've learned them in the U.S. There are several common verbs which often have "T" endings in Britain which seem a little quaint and poetic in American English, where we prefer "-ED." Other examples: "dreamt/dreamed," "dwelt/dwelled," "leant/leaned," "leapt/leaped," and "spelt/spelled." However, the following alternatives are both in the U.S.: "burned/burnt" and "kneeled/knelt."

E / I

The familiar rule is the English words are spelled with the "I" before the "E" unless they follow a "C," as in "receive." But it is important to add that words in which the vowel sound is an "A" like "neighbor" and "weigh" are also spelled with the "E" first. And there are a few exceptions like "counterfeit," seize, and "weird."

Either

"Either" often gets misplaced in a sentence: "He either wanted to build a gambling casino or a convent" should be "He wanted to build either a gambling casino or a convent." Put "either" just before the first thing being compared.

Either are/Either is

As a subject, "either" is singular. It's s the opposite of "both," and refers to one at a time: "Either ketchup or mustard is good on a hot dog." But is "either" is modifying a subject in an "either.......or" phrase, then the number of the verb is determined by the number of the second noun: "Either the puppy or the twins seem to need my attention every other minute."

Elapse/Lapse

Both these words come from a Latin root meaning "to slip." "Elapse" almost always refers to the passage of time. "Lapse" usually refers to a change of state, as in lapsing from consciousness into unconsciousness. Here are examples of the correct uses of these words you might get in the mail: "Six months have elapsed since your last dental appointment" and "You have allowed your subscription to Bride Magazine to lapse." Occasionally "lapse" can be used as a synonym of "elapse" in the sense "to slip away." Substituting one for the other is dangerous, however, if you are a lawyer. Insurance policies and collective bargaining agreements do not elapse when they expire, they lapse.

Electrocute/Shock

To electrocute is to kill using electricity. If you live to tell the tale, you've been shocked, but not electrocuted. For the same reason, the phrase "electrocuted to death" is a redundancy.

Elicit/Illicit

The lawyer tries to elicit a description of the attacker from the witness. "Elicit" is always a verb. "Illicit," in contrast, is always an adjective describing something illegal or naughty.

Embaress/Embarrass

You can pronounce the last two syllables as two distinct words as a jog to memory, except that then the word may be misspelled "embareass," which isn't right either. You also have to remember the double R: "embarrass.

Energent/Emergency

The error of considering "emergent" to be the adjectival form of "emergency" is common only in medical writing, but it is becoming widespread. "Emergent" properly means "emerging" and normally refers to events that are just beginning—barely noticeable rather than catastrophic. "Emergency" is an adjective as well as a noun, so rather than writing "emergent care," use the homely "emergency care."

Emigrate/Immigrate

To "emigrate" is to live a country. The E at the beginning of the word is related to the E in other words having to do with going out, such as "exit." "Immigrate," in contrast, looks as if it might have something to do with going in, and indeed it does: it means to move into a new country. The same distinction applies to "emigration" and "immigration."

Note the double M in the second form. A migrant is someone who continually moves about.

Eminent/Imminent/Immanent

By far the most common of these is "eminent," meaning "prominent, famous." "Imminent," in phrases like "facing imminent disaster," means "threatening." It comes from Latin minere, meaning "to project or overhang." Think of a mine threatening to cave in. Positive events can also be imminent: they just need to be coming soon. The rarest of the three is "immanent," used by philosophers to mean "inherent" and by theologians to mean "present throughout the universe" when referring to God. It comes from Latin "maner," "remain." Think of God creating "man" in his own image.

Empathy/Sympathy

If you think you fel just like another person, you are feeling empathy. If you just feel sorry for another person, you're feeling sympathy.

Emphasize On/Emphasize

You can place emphasis on something, or you can emphasize it, but you can't emphasize on it or stress on it, though you can place on it.

Enormity/Enormousness

Originally these two words were synonymous, but 'enormity' got whittled down to meaning something monstrous or outrageous. Don't wonder at the "enormity" of the place of Versailles unless you wish to express horror at this embodiment of Louis XIV' sego. "Enormity" can also be used as a noun meaning "monstrosity."

End Result/End

Usually a redundancy. Most of the time plain "result" will do fine.

Enquire/Inquire

These are alternative spellings of the same word. "Enquire" is perhaps slightly more common in the U.K., but either is acceptable in the most U.S.

Enthuse

"Enthuse" is a handy word and "state enthusiastically" is not nearly so striking; but unfortunately "enthuse" is not acceptable in the most formal contexts.

Envelop/Envelope

To warp something up in a covering is to envelop it (pronounced "enVELLup"). The specific wrapping you put around a letter is an envelope (pronounced variously, but with the accent on the first syllable).

Envious/Jealous

Although these are often treated as synonyms, there is a difference. You are envious of what others have that you lack. Jealousy, on the other hand, involves wanting to hold on the what you do have. You can be jealous of your boyfriend's attraction to other women, but you're envious of your boyfriend's CD collection.

Enviroment/Environment

The second N in "environment" is seldom pronounced distinctly, so it's not surprising that is often omitted in writing. If you know the related word "environs" it may help remind you.

Epigram/Epigraph/Epitaph/Epithet

An epigram is a pithy saying, usually humorous. Mark Twain was responsible for many striking, mostly cynical epigrams, such as "Always do right. That will gratify some of the people, and astonish the rest." Unfortunately, he was also responsible for an even more campus one that has been confusion people ever since: "Everyone is a moon, and has a dark side which he never shows to anybody." It's true that the moon keeps one side away form the earth, but—if you don't count the faint glow reflected from the earth—it is not any darker than the side that faces us. In fact, over time, the side caching us is darkened slightly more often because it is occasionally eclipsed by the shadow of the earth.

An epigraph is a brief quotation used to introduce a piece of writing or the inscription on a statue or building.

An epitaph is the inscription on a tombstone or some other tribute to a dead person.

In literature, an epithet is a term that replaces or is added to the name of a person, like "clear-eyed Athena," in which "clear-eyed" is the epithet. You are more likely to encounter the term in its negative sense, as a term of insult or abuse: "the shoplifter hurled epithets at the guard who had arrested her."

Epitiomy/Epitome

Nothing makes you look quite so foolish as spelling a sophisticated word incorrectly. Taken directly from Latin, where it means "abridgement," "epitome" is now most often used to designate an extremely representative example of the general class: "Snow white is the epitome of a Disney cartoon feature." Those who don't misspell this word often mispronounce it, misled by its spelling, as "EP-i-tohm," but the proper pronunciation is "ee-PIT-o-mee. "The word means "essence," not "climax" so instead of writing "the market had reached the epitome of frenzied selling at noon," use "peak" or a similar word.

Every

"Every," "everybody" and "everyone" and related expressions are normally treated as singular in American English: "Every woman I ask out tells me she already has plans for Saturday nigh." However, constructions like "everyone brought their own lunch" are widely accepted now because of a desire to avoid specifying "his" or "her." See "they/their (singular)."

Everyday

"Everyday" is a perfectly good adjective, as in "I'm most comfortable in my everyday cothes." The problem comes when people turn the adverbial phrase" "every day" into a single word. It is incorrect to write "I take a shower everyday." It should be "I take a shower every day."

Everytime/Every Time

"Every time" is always two separate words.

Evidence to/Evidence of

You can provide evidence to a court, even enough evidence to convict someone; but the standard expression "is evidence of" "requires "of" rather than "to" in sentences like this: "Driving through the front entrance of the Burger king is evidence of Todd' inexperience in driving." If you could substitute "evidences" or "evidenced" in your sentence, you need "of."

Exact same/exactly the same

In casual speech we often say things like, "The fruitcake he have me was the exact same one I" d given him last Christmas, "but in formal English the phrase is "exactly the same."

Exalt/Exult

When you celebrate joyfully, you exult. When you raise something high (even if only in your opinion), you exalt it. Neither word has an "H" in it.

Excape/escape

The proper spelling is "escape." Say it that way too.

Exceptional/exceptionable

If you take exception (object) to something, you find it "exceptionable." The more common word is "exceptional," applied to things that are out of the ordinary, usually in a positive way: "these are exceptional Buffalo wings."

Exhileration/Exhilaration

"Exhilaration" is closely related to "hilarious," whose strongly accented A should help remind you of the correct spelling.

Expresses that/says that

"In her letter Jane expresses that she is getting irritated with me for not writing" should be corrected to "In her letter Jane says that—"

You can express an idea or a thought, but you can't ever express that. In technical terms, "express" is a transitive verb and requires an object.

Expresso/espresso

I've read several explanations of the origin of this word: the coffee is made expressly for you upon your order, or the steam is expressed through the grounds, or (as most people suppose—and certainly wrongly) the coffee is made at express speed. One thing is certain: the word is "espresso," not "expresso."

While you're at an American espresso stand, you might muse on the fact that both "biscotti" and "panini" are plural forms, but you're likely to baffle the barista if you ask in correct Italian for a biscotti or a panino.

In the fact that/by the fact that

The correct phrase is "by the fact that," not "in the fact that." While we're at it, "infact" is not a word; "in fact" is always a two-word phrase.

Fair/Fare

When you send your daughter off to camp, you hope she"ll fare well. That's way you bid her a fond farewell. "Fair" as a verb is a rare word meaning "to smooth a surface to prepare it for being joined to another."

Farther/Further

Some authorities (like the Associated Press) insist on "farther" to refer to physical distance and on "further" to refer to an extent of time or degree, but others treat the two words as interchangeable except for insisting on "further" for "in addition," and "moreover." You"ll always be safe in making the distinction; some people get really testy about this.

Fastly/Fast

"Fastly" is an old form that has died out in English. Interest in soccer is growing fast, not "fastely."

Fatal/Fateful

A "fatal" event is a deadly one; a "fateful" one is determined by fate. If there are no casualties left lying at the scene—whether mangled corpses or failed negotiations—the word you are seeking is "fateful." The latter word also has many positive uses, such as "George fondly remembered that fateful night in which he first met the woman he was to love to his dying day."

Faze/Phase

"Faze" means to embarrass or disturb, but is almost always used in the negative sense, as in "the fact that the overhead projector bulb was burned out didn't faze her." "Phase" is a noun or verb having to do with an aspect of something. "He's just going through a temperamental phase." "They're going to phase in the new accounting procedures gradually." Unfortunately, Star Trek has confused matters by calling its ray pistols phasers. Too bad they aren't fazers instead.

Fearful/Fearsome

To be "fearful" is to be afraid. To be "fearsome" is to cause fear in others. Remember that someone who is fierce is fearsome rather than fearful.

Febuary/February

Few people pronounce the first R in "February" distinctly, so it is not surprising that it is often omitted in spelling. This poor month is short on days; don't further impoverish it by robbing it of one of its letters.

Firey/Fiery

It's "fire," so why isn't it "firey"? If you listen closely, you hear that "fire" has two distinct vowel sounds in it: "fi-er." Spelling the adjective "fiery" helps to preserve that double sound.

Finalize/Finish, Put into final form

"Finalize" is very popular among bureaucrats, but many people hate it. Avoid it unless you know that everyone in your environment uses it too.

Fiscal/Physical

The middle syllable of "physical" is often omitted in pronunciation, making it sound like the unrelated word "fiscal." Sound that unaccented "I" distinctly.

Fit The Bill/Fill The Bill

Originally a "bill" was any piece of writing, especially a legal document (we still speak of bills being introduced into Congress in this sense). More narrowly, it also came to man a list such as a restaurant "bill of fare" (menu) or an advertisement listing attractions in a theatrical variety show such as might be posted on a "billboard." In nineteenth-century America, when producers found short acts to supplement the main attractions, nicely filling out an evening' s entertainment, they were said in a rhyming phrase to "fill the bill." People who associate bill principally with shipping invoices frequently transform this expression, meaning "to meet requirements or desires," into "fit the bill." They are thinking of bills as if they were orders, lists of requirements. It is both more logical and more traditional to say "fill the bill."

Flair/Flare

"Flair" is conspicuous talent: "She has a flair for organization." "Flare" is either a noun meaning "flame" or a verb meaning to blaze with light or to burst into anger.

Flammable/Inflammable

The prefix "in-" does not indicate negation here; it comes from the word "inflame." "Flammable" and inflammable" both mean "easy to catch on fire"; but so many people misunderstand the latter term that it's better to stick with "flammable" in safety warnings.

Flaunt/Flout

To flaunt is to show off: you flaunt your new necklace by wearing it to work. "Flout" has a more negative connotation; it means to treat with contempt some rule or standard. The cliché is "to flout convention." Flaunting may be in bad taste because it's ostentatious, but it is not a violation of standards.

Flesh out/Flush out

To "flesh out" an idea is to give it substance, as a sculptor adds clay flesh to a skeletal armature. To "flush out" a criminal is to drive him or her out into the open. The latter term is derived from bird-hunting, in which one flushes, out a covey of quail. If you are trying to develop something further, use "flesh"; but if you are trying to reveal something hitherto concealed, use "flush."

Floppy Disk/Hard Disk

Floppy disks are fast disappearing form the computer world, but it's been many years since they were literally floppy. The fact that a ½" diskette is enclosed in a hard plastic case should not lead you to call it a "hard disk." That's a high-capacity storage medium like the main disk inside you computer on which your programs, operating system, and data are stored.

Flounder/Founder

As a verb, "founder" means "to fill with water and sink." It is also used metaphorically of various kinds of equally catastrophic failures. In contrast, to flounder is to thrash about in the water (like a flounder), struggling to stay alive. "Flounder" is also often used metaphorically to indicate various sorts of desperate struggle. If you're sunk, you've foundered. If you're still struggling, you're floundering.

Foot/Feet

You can use eight-foot boards to side a house, but "foot" is correct only in this sort of adjectival phrase combined with a number (and usually hyphenated). The boards are eight feet (not foot) long. It's always X feet per second and X feet away.

Footnotes/Endnotes

About that time that computers began to make the creation and printing of footnotes extremely simple and cheap, style manuals began to urge a shift away from them to endnotes printed at the ends of chapters or at the end of a book or paper rather than at the foot of the page. I happen o think this was a big mistake; but in any case, if you are using endnotes, don't call them "footnotes."

For/Fore/Four

The most common member of this trio is the preposition "for," which is not a problem for most people. "Fore" always has to do with the front of something (it's what you shout to warn someone when you've sent a golf ball their way). "Four" is just the number "4."

For All intensive purposes/For all intents and purposes

Another example of the oral transformation of language by people who don't read much. "For all intents and purposes" is an old cliché which won't thrill anyone, but using the mistaken alternative is likely to elicit guffaws.

For Free/Free

Some people object to "for free" because any sentence containing the phrase will read just as well without the "for," but it is standard English.

For one/For one Thing

People often say "for one" when they mean "for one thing": "I really want to go to the movie. For one, Kevin Spacey is my favorite actor." (One what?) The only time you should use "for one" by itself to give an example of something is when you have earlier mentioned a class to which the example belongs: "There are a lot of reasons I don't want you old car. For one, there are squirrels living in the upholstery." (One reason.)

For Sale/On Sale

If you're selling something, it's for sale; but if you lower the price, it goes on sale.

Forbidding/Foreboding/Formidable

"Foreboding" means "ominous," as in "The sky was a foreboding shade of gray" (i.e. predictive of a storm). The prefix "fore-" with an E, often indicates futurity, e.g. "forecast," "foreshadowing" and "foreword" (a prefatory bit of writing at the beginning of a book, often misspelled "forward"). A forbidding person or task is hostile or dangerous: "The trek across the desert to the nearest latte stand was for forbidding." The two are easily confused because some things, like storms, can be both foreboding and forbidding.

"Formidable," which originally meant "fear-inducing" ("Mike Tyson is a formidable opponent") has come to be used primarily as a compliment meaning "awe-inducing" ("Gary Kasparov's formidable skills as a chess player were of no avail against Deep blue").

Forceful, Forcible, Forced

These words sometimes overlap, but generally "forceful" means "Powerful" ("He imposed his forceful personality on the lion.") while" forcible" must be used instead to describe the use of force ("The burglar made a forcible entry into the apartment). "Forced" is often used for the latter purpose, but some prefer to reserve this word to describe something that is done or decided upon as a result of outside causes without necessarily being violent: "a forced landing, " "a forced smile," "forced labor."

Forego/Forgo

The E in "forego" tells you it has to do with going before. It occurs mainly in the expression "foregone conclusion," a conclusion arrived at in advance. "Forgo" means to abstain from or do without. "After finishing his steak, he decided to forgo the blueberry cheesecake."

Formally/Formerly

These two are often mixed up in speech. If you are doing something in a formal manner, you are behaving formally; but if you previously behaved differently, you did so formerly.

Foresee/Forsee

"Foresee" means "to see into the future." There are lots of words with the prefix "fore—" which are future-oriented, including "foresight," "foretell," "forethought," and "foreword," all of which are often misspelled by people who omit the E. Just remember: what golfers shout when they are warning people ahead of them about the shot they are about to make is "fore!"

Fortuitous/Fortunate

"Fortuitous" events happen by chance, they need not be fortunate events, only random one: It was purely fortuitous that the meter reader came along five minutes before I returned to my car." Although fortunate events may be fortuitous, when you mean "Lucky," use "fortunate."

Foul/Fowl

A chicken is a fowl. A poke in the eye is a foul.

Mount fujiyama/Fujiyama

"Yama" means "mountain" in Japanese, so when you say "Mount Fujiyama" you are saying "Mount Fuji Mountain." The Japanese usually say "Fuji-san"; but "Fujiyama," or "Mount Fuji" is standard in English—just be aware that both sound 'foreign' to Japanese native speakers.

-Ful/-Fuls

It's one cupful, but two cupfuls, not "two cupsful." The same goes for "spoonfuls" and "glassful."

Fulsome

Because its most common use is in the phrase "fulsome praise," many people suppose that this word means something like "generous" or "whole-hearted." Actually, it means "disgusting," and "fulsome praise" is disgustingly exaggerated praise.

G/Q

Lower-case "q" is the mirror image of lower-case "g" in many typefaces, and the two are often confused with each other and the resulting misspelling missed in proofreading, for instance "quilt" when "guilt" is intended.

Gaff/Gaffe

"Gaffe" is a French word meaning "embarrassing mistake," and should not be mixed up with "gaff": a large hook.

Gamut/Gauntlet

To "run a gamut" is to go through the whole scale or spectrum of something. To "run the gauntlet" (also gantlet) is to run between two lines of people who are trying to beat you. And don't confuse "gamut" with "gambit," a play in chess, and by extension, a tricky maneuver of any kind.

Guard/Guard

Too bad the Elizabethan "guard" won out over the earlier, French-derived spelling "grade"; but the word was never spelled "guard." The standard spelling is related to Italian and Spanish "guard," pronounced "guard."

Ghandi/Gandhi

Mohandas K. Gandhi's name has an H after the D, not after the G. Note that "Mahatma" ("great soul") is an honorific title, not actually part of his birth name.

Gibe/Jibe/Jive

"Give" is a now rare term meaning "to tease." "Jibe" means "to agree," but is usually used negatively, as in "the alibis of the two crooks didn't jibe." The latter word is often confused with "Jive," which derives from slang which originally meant to treat in a jazzy manner ("Jivin" the Blues A way") but also came to be associated with deception ("Don't give me any of that jive").

Gig/Jig

"The jig is up" is an old slang expression meaning "the game is over—we're caught." A musician's job is a gig.

Gild/Guild

You gild an object by covering it with gold; you can join an organization like the theatre guild.

God

When "God" is the name of a god, as in Judaism, Christianity and Islam ("Allah" is just Arabic for "God," and many modern

Muslims translate the name when writing in English), it needs to be capitalized like any other name. When it is used as a generic term, as in "He looks like a Greek god," it is not capitalized.

If you see the word rendered "G*d" or "G-d" it's not an error, but a Jewish writer reverently following the orthodox prohibition against spelling out the name of the deity in full.

Gone/Went

This is one of those cases in which a common word has a past participle which is not formed by the simple addition of –ED and which often trip people up. "I should have went to the business meeting, but the game was tied in the ninth" should be "I should have gone—"The same problem crops up with the two forms of the verb "to do." Say "I should have done my taxes before the IRS "called" rather than "I should have did..."

Good/Well

"Good" is the adjective; "well" is the adverb. You do something well, but you give someone something good. The exception is verbs of sensation in phrases such as "the pie smells good," or "I feel good." Despite the arguments of nigglesis, this is standard usage. Saying "the pie smells well" would imply that the pastry in question had a nose. Similarly, "I feel well" is also acceptable, especially when discussing health; but it is not the only correct usage.

Got/Gotten

In England, the old word "gotten" dropped out of use except in such stock phrases as "ill-gotten" and "gotten up," but in the U.S. it is frequently used as the past participle of "get." Sometimes the two are interchangeable. However, "got" implies current possession, as in "I've got just five dollars to buy my dinner with." "Gotten," in contrast, often implies the process of getting hold of something: "I've gotten five dollars for cleaning out Mrs. Quimby's shed" emphasizing the earning of the money rather than its possession. Phrases that involve some sort of process usually involve "gotten": "My grades have gotten better since I moved out of the fraternity." When you have to leave, you've got to go. If you say you've "gotten to go" you're implying someone gave you permission to go.

Graduate/Graduate from

In certain dialects (notably that of New York City) it is common to say "he is going to graduate school in June" rather than the more standard "graduate from." When writing for a national or international audience, use the "from."

Grammer/Grammar

It's amazing how many people write to thank me for helping them with their "grammar." It's "grammar." The word is often incorrectly used to label patterns of spelling and usage that have nothing to do with the structure of language, the proper subject of grammar in the most conservative sense. Not all bad writing is due to bad grammar.

Gratis/Gratuitous

If you do something nice without being paid, you do it "gratis." Technically, such a deed can also be "gratuitous"; but if you do or say something obnoxious and uncalled for, it's always "gratuitous," not "gratis."

Greatful/Grateful

Your appreciation may be great, but you express gratitude by being grateful.

Grievious/Grievous

There are just two syllables in "grievous," and it's pronounced "grieve-us."

Grisly/Grizzly

"Grisly" means "horrible", a "grizzly" is a bear. "The grizzly left behind the grisly remains of his victim." "Grizzled," means "having gray hairs," not to be confused with "gristly," full of gristle.

Gyp/Cheat

Gypsies complain that "gyp" ("cheat") reflects bias; but the word is so well entrenched and its origin so obscure to most users that there is little hope of eliminating it from standard use any time soon.

Hairbrained/Harebrained

Although "hairbrained" is common, the original word "harebrained," means "silly as a hare" (rabbit) and is preferred in writing.

Hardly Never/Hardly Ever

The expression is "hardly ever."

Hardy/Dearty

These two words overlap somewhat, usually the word you want is "hearty." The standard expressions are "a hearty appetite," "a hearty weal," a "hearty handshake," "a hearty welcome," and "hearty applause." Something difficult to kill is described as a "hardy perennial," but should not be substituted for "hearty" in the other expressions. "Party hearty" and "party hardy" are both common renderings of a common youth saying, but the first makes more sense.

Heading/Bound

If you're reporting on traffic conditions, it's redundant to say "heading northbound on 1-5." It's it's either "heading north" or "northbound."

Hearing-Impaired/Deaf

"Hearing-impaired" is not an all-purpose substitute for "deaf" since it strongly implies some residual ability to hear.

"HIV" Virus

"HIV" stands for "human immunodeficiency virus," so adding the word "virus" to the acronym creates a redundancy. "HIV" is the name of the organism that is the cause of AIDS,not, not a name for the disease itself. A person may be HIV-positive (a test shows the person to be infected with the virus) without having yet developed AIDS (acquired immunodeficiency syndrome). HIV is the cause, AIDS the result.

Hanged/Hung

Originally these words were pretty much interchangeable, but "hanged" eventually came to be used pretty exclusively to mean "executed by hanging." Does nervousness about the existence of an indelicate adjectival form of the word prompt people to avoid the correct word in such sentences as "Lady wrothley saw to it that her ancestors" portraits were properly hung"? Nevertheless, "hung" is correct except when capital punishment is being imposed.

Hear/Here

If you find yourself writing sentences like "I know I left my wallet hear!" you shold note that "hear" has the word "ear" buried in it and let that remind you that it refers only to hearing and is always a verb (except when you are giving the British cheer "Hear! Hear") " I left my wallet here" is the correct expression.

He don't/He Doesn't

In formal English, "don't" is not used in the third person singular. "I don't like avocado ice·cream" is correct, and so is "they don't have their passports yet "and "they don't have the sense to come in out of the rain"; but "he don't have no money," though common in certain dialects, is nonstandard on two counts: it should be "he doesn't" and "any money." The same is true of other forms: "she don't" and "it don't" Should be "she doesn't" and "it doesn't."

Heighth/Height

"Width" has a "TH" at the end, so why doesn't "height"? In fact it used to, but the standard pronunciation today ends in a plain "T" sound. People who use the obsolete form misspell it as well, so pronunciation is no guide. By the way, this is one of those pesky exceptions to the rule, "I before E except after C," but the vowels are seldom switched, perhaps because we see it printed on so many forms along with "age" and "weight."

Help The Problem

People say they want to help the problem of poverty when what they really mean is that they want to help solve the problem of poverty. Poverty flourishes without any extra help, thank you. I guess I know what a "suicide help line" is, but I" d rather it were a "suicide prevention help line." I suppose it's too late to ask people to rename alcoholism support groups as sobriety support groups, but it's a shoddy sue of language.

Hero/Protagonist

In ordinary usage "hero" has two meanings: "leading character in a story" and "brave, admirable person." In simple tales the two meanings may work together, but in modern literature and film the leading character or "protagonist" (a technical term common in literary criticism) may behave in a very unheroic fashion. Students who express shock that the "hero' of a play or novel behaves despicably reveal their inexperience. In literature classes avoid the word unless you mean to stress a character's heroic qualities. However, if you are discussing the main character in a traditional opera, where values are often simple, you may get by with referring to the male lead as the "hero"—but is Don Giovanni really a hero?

Heroin/Heroine

Heroin is a highly addictive opium derivative; the main female character in a narrative is a heroine.

Highly Looked upon/Highly Regarded

Many people, struggling to come up with phrase "highly regarded," come up with the awkward "highly looked upon" instead; which suggests that the looker is placed in a high position, looking down, when what is meant is that the looker is looking up to someone or something admirable.

Him, Her/He She

There is a group of personal pronouns to be used as subjects in a sentence, including "he," "she," "I," and "we." Then there is a separate group of object pronouns, including "him," "her", "me" and "us." The problem is that the folks who tend to mix up the two sets often don't find the subject/object distinction clear or helpful, and say things like "Her and me went to the movies."

A simple test is to substitute "us" for "her and me." Would you say "us went to the movies?" obviously not. You'd normally say "we went to the movies," so when "we" is broken into the two persons involved it becomes "She and I went to the movies."

But you would say "the murder scene scared us," so it's correct to say "the murder scene scared her and me."

If you aren't involve, use "they" and "them" as test words instead of "us" and "we." "They won the lottery" becomes "he and she won the lottery," and "the check was mailed to them" becomes "the check was mailed to him and her."

Hippie/Hippy

A long-haired 60s flower child was a "hippie." "Hippy" is an adjective describing someone with wide hips. The IE is not caused by a Y changing to IE in the plural as in "puppy" and "puppies." It is rather a dismissive diminutive, invented by older, more sophisticated hipsters looking down on the new kids as mere "hippies." Confusing these two is definitely unhip.

Hisself/Himself

In some dialects people say "hisself" for "himself," but this is nonstandard.

An Historic/A Historic

You should use "an" before a word beginning with an "H" only if the "H" is not pronounced: "an honest effort"; it's properly "a historic event" though many sophisticated speakers somehow prefer the sound of "an historic," So that version is not likely to get you into any real trouble.

Hoard/Horde

A greedily hoarded treasure is a hoard. A herd of wildebeests or a mob of people is a horde.

Hone In/Home in

You home in on a target (the center of the target is "home"). "Honing" has to do with sharpening knives, not aim.

How Come/Why

"How come?" is a common questioning casual speech, but in formal contexts use "why"

Hyphens & Dashes

Dashes are longer than hyphens, but since some browsers do not reliably interpret the code for dashes, they are usually rendered on the Web as they were on old-fashioned typewriters, as double hyphens—like that. Dashes tend to separate elements and hyphens to link them. Few people would substitute a dash for a hyphen in an expression like "a quick-witted scoundrel," but the opposite is common. In a sentence like "Astrud—unlike Inger—enjoyed vacations in Spain rather than England," one often sees hyphens incorrectly substituted for dashes.

When you are typing for photocopying or direct printing, it is a good idea to learn how to type a true dash instead of the double hyphen (computers differ). In old-fashioned styles, dashes (but never hyphens) are surrounded by spaces—like this. With modern computer output which emulates professional printing, this makes little sense. Skip the spaces unless your editor or teacher insists on them.

There are actually two kinds of dashes. The most common is the "em-dash" (theoretically the width of a letter "M—but this is often not the case). To connect numbers, it is traditional to use an "en-dash" which is somewhat shorter, but not as short as a hyphen: "cocktails 5-7 pm." All modern computers can produce en-dashes, but few people know how to type them. For most purposes you don't have to worry about them, but if you are preparing material for print, you should learn how to use them.

Hysterical/Hilarious

People say of a bit of humor or a comical situation that it was "hysterical"—shorthand for "hysterically funny"—meaning "hilarious." But when you speak of a man being "hysterical" it means he is having a fit of hysteria, and that may not be funny at all.

I/Me/Myself

In the old days when people studied traditional grammar, we could simply say, "The first person singular pronoun is "I" when it's a subject and "me" when it's an object," but now few people know what that means. Let's see if we can apply some common sense here. The misuse of "I" and "myself" for "me" is caused by nervousness about "me." Educated people know that "Jim and me is goin" down to slop the hogs," is not elegant speech, not "correct." It should be "Jim and I" because if I were slopping the hogs alone I would never say "Me is going—" So far so good. But the notion that there is something wrong with "me" leads people to overcorrect and avoid it where it is perfectly appropriate. People will say "The document had to be signed by both Susan and I" when the correct statement would be, "The document had to be signed by both Susan and me. "Trying even harder to avoid the lowly "me," many people will substitute "myself," as in "The suspect uttered epithets at Officer O" Leary and myself." "Myself" is no better than "I" as an object. "Myself" is not a sort of all-purpose intensive form of "me" or "I." Use "myself" only when you have used "I" earlier in the same sentence: "I am not particularly fond of goat cheese myself." "I kept half the loot for myself." All this confusion can easily be avoided if you just remove the second party from the sentences where you feel tempted to use "myself" as an object or feel nervous about "me." You wouldn't say, "The IRS sent the refund check to I," so you shouldn't say "The IRS sent the refund check to my wife and I" either. And you shouldn't say "to my wife and myself." "The only correct way to say this is, The IRS sent the refund check to my wife and me." Still sounds too casual? Get over it.

On a related point, those who continue to announce "It is I" have traditional grammatical correctness on their side, but they are vastly outnumbered by those who proudly boast "it's me!" There's not much that can be done about this now. Similarly, if a caller asks for Susan and Susan answers "This is she," her somewhat antiquated correctness is likely to startle the questioner into confusion.

-IC

In the Cold War era, anti-socialists often accused their enemies of being "socialistic" by which they meant that although they were not actually socialists, some of their beliefs were like those of socialists. But the "-ic" suffix is recklessly used in all kinds of settings, often without understanding its implications. Karl Marx was not "socialistic," he was actually socialist.

Ida/Ideal

Any thought can be an idea, but only the best ideas worth pursuing are ideals.

If I was/If I were

The subjunctive mood, always weak in English, has been dwindling away for centuries until it has almost vanished. According to rational though, statements about the conditional future such as "If I were a carpenter...." require the subjunctive "were"; but "was" is certainly much more common. Still, if you want to impress those in the know with your usage use "were." The same goes for other pronouns: "you," "she," "he," and "it." In the case of the plural pronouns "we" and "they" the form "was" is definitely nonstandard, of course, because it is a singular form.

Ignorant/Stupid

A person can be ignorant (not knowing some fact or idea) without being stupid (incapable of learning because of a basic mental deficiency). And those who say, "That's an ignorant idea" when they mean "stupid idea" are expressing their own ignorance.

Immaculate conception/Virgin Birth

The doctrine of "immaculate conception" (the belief that Mary was conceived without inheriting original sin) is often confused with the doctrine of the "virgin birth" (the belief that Mary gave birth to Jesus while remaining a virgin).

Impertinent/Irrelevant

"Impertinent" looks as if it ought to mean the opposite of "pertinent," and indeed it once did; but for centuries now its meaning in ordinary speech has been narrowed to "impudent," specifically in regard to actions or speech toward someone regarded as socially superior. Only snobs and very old-fashioned people use "impertinent" correctly; most people would be well advised to forget it and use "irrelevant" instead to mean the opposite of "pertinent."

Imply/infer

These two words, which originally had quite distinct meanings, have become so blended together that most people no longer distinguish between them. If you want to avoid irritating the rest of us, use "imply" when something is being suggested without being explicitly stated and "infer" when someone is trying to arrive at a conclusion based on evidence. "Imply" is more assertive, active: I imply that you need to revise your paper; and, based on my hints, you infer that I didn't think highly of your first draft.

In regards to/With Regard to

Business English is deadly enough without scrambling it. "As regards your downsizing plan——" is acceptable, if stiff. "In regard to—" is also correct. But don't confuse the two by writing "In regards to."

In the Fact that/In that

Many people mistakenly write "in the fact that" when they mean simply "in the" in sentences like "It seemed wiser not to go to work in the fact that the boss had discovered the company picnic money was missing." Omit "the fact." While we're at it, "infact" is not a word; "in fact" is always a two-word phrase.

Incent, Incentivize

Business folks sometimes use "incent" to mean "create an incentive," but it's not standard English. "Incentivize" is even more widely used, but strikes many people as an ugly substitute for "encourage."

Incidence/Incidents/Instances

These three overlap in meaning just enough to confuse a lot of people few of us have a need for "incidence, "which most often refers to degree or extent of the occurrence of something ("the incidence of measles in Whitman County has dropped markedly since the vaccine has been provided free"). "Incidents," which is pronounced identically, is merely the plural of "incident," meaning "occurrences" ("police reported damage to three different outhouses in separate incidents last Halloween"). Instances are examples ("semicolons are not required in the first three instances given in your query"). Incidents can be used as instances only if someone is using them as examples.

Indepth/In Depth

You can make an "in-depth" study of a subject by studying it "in depth," but never "indepth." Like "a lot" this is two words often mistaken for one. The first, adjectival, use of the phrase given above is commonly hyphenated, which may lead some people to splice the words even more closely together. "Indepth" is usually used as an adverb by people of limited vocabulary who would be better off saying "profoundly" or "thoroughly." Some of them go so far as to say that they have studied a subject "indepthly." Avoid this one if you don't want to be snickered at.

Indian/Native American

Although academics have long promoted "Native American" as a more accurate lable than "Indian," most of the people so labeled continue to refer to themselves as "Indians" and prefer that term. In Canada, there is a move to refer to descendants of the original inhabitants as "First peoples," but so far that has not spread to the U.S.

Individual/Person

Law-enforcement officers often use "individual" as a simple synonym for "person" when they don't particularly mean to stress individuality: "I pursued the individual who had fired the weapon at me for three block." This sort of use of "individual" lends an oddly formal air to your writing. When "person" works as well, use it.

Infamous/Notorious

"Infamous" means famous in a bad way. It is related to the word "infamy." Humorists have for a couple of centuries jokingly used the word in a positive sense, but the effectiveness of the joke depends on the listener knowing that this is a misuse of the term. Because this is a very old joke indeed you should stick to using "infamous" only of people like Hitler and Billy the kid.

"Notorious" means the same thing as "infamous" and should also only be used in a negative sense.

Infact/In fact

"In fact" is always two words.

Install/Instill

People conjure up visions of themselves as upgradable robots when they write things like "My Aunt Tillie tried to install the spirit of giving in my heart." The word they are searching for is "instill." You install equipment, you instill feelings or attitudes.

Instances/Instants

Brief moments are "instants," and examples of anything are "instances."

Interface/Interact

The use of the computer term "interface" as a verb, substituting for "interact," is widely objected to.

Interment/Internment

Interment is burial; internment is merely imprisonment.

Internet/Intranet

"Internet" is the proper name of the network most people connect to, and the word needs to be capitalized. However "intranet," a network confined to a smaller group, is a generic term which does not deserve capitalization. In advertising, we often read things like "unlimited internet, $19." It would be more accurate to refer in this sort of context to "internet access."

Interpretate/Interpret

"Interpretate" is mistakenly formed from "interpretation," but the verb form is simply "interpret." See also "orientate."

Into/In to

"Into" is a preposition which often answers the question, "where?" For example, "Tom and Becky had gone far into the cave before they realized they were lost." Sometimes the "where" is metaphorical, as in, "he went into the army" or "She went into business." It can also refer by analogy to time: "The snow lingered on the ground well into April." In old-fashioned math talk, it could be used to refer to division: "two into six is three." In other instances where the words "in" and "to" just happen to find themselves neighbors, they must remain separate words. For instance, "Rachel dived back in to rescue the struggling boy." Here "to" belongs with "rescue" and means "in order to," not "where." (If the phrase had been "dived back into the water," "into" would be required.)

Try speaking the sentence concerned aloud, pausing distinctly between "in" and "to." If the result sounds wrong, you probably need "into"

Then there is the 60s colloquialism which lingers on in which "into" means "deeply interested or involved in": "Kevin is into baseball cards. " This is derived from usages like "the committee is looking into the fund-raising scandal." The abbreviated form is not acceptable formal English, but is quite common in informal communications.

Ironically/Coincidentally

An event that is strikingly different from or the opposite of what one would have expected, usually producing a sense of incongruity, is ironic: "The sheriff proclaimed a zero-tolerance policy on drugs, but ironically flunked his own test." Other striking comings-together of events lacking these qualities are merely coincidental: "the lovers leapt off the tower just as a hay wagon coincidentally happened to be passing below."

Irregardless/Regardless

Regardless of what you have heard, "irregardless" is a redundancy. The suffix "-less" on the end of the word already makes the word negative. It doesn't need the negative prefix "Ir-" added to make it even more negative.

Is, is

In speech, people often lose track in the middle of a sentence and repeat "is" instead of saying "that": "The problem with the conflict in the Balkans is, is the ethnic tensions seem exacerbated by everything we do," This is just a nervous tic, worth being alert against when you're speaking publicly.

Of course, I suppose it all depends on what you think the meaning of "is" is.

Islams/Muslims

Followers of Islam are called "Muslims," not "Islams." (Although the Associated press still does not accept it, "Muslim" is now widely preferred over the older and less phonetically accurate "Moslem.")

Isreal/Israel

To remember how to spell "Israel" properly, try pronouncing it the way Israelis do when they're speaking English: "ISS-rah-el."

Issues/Problems

In many circles people speak of "having issues" when they mean they have problems with some issue or objections of some kind. Traditionalists are annoyed by this.

Itch/Scratch

Strictly speaking, you scratch an itch. If you're trying to get rid of a tingly feeling on your back scratch it, don't itch it.

Its/It's

The exception to the general rule that one should use an apostrophe to indicate possession is in possessive pronouns. Some of them are not a problem, "Mine" has no misleading "s" at the end to invite an apostrophe. And few people are tempted to write "hi" s," though the equally erroneous "her" s" fairly common, as are "our" s" and "their" s"—all wrong, wrong, wrong. The problem with avoiding "it's" as a possessive is that this spelling is perfectly correct as a contraction meaning "it is." Just remember two points and you'll never make this mistake again. (1) "it's" always means "it is" or "it has" and nothing else. (2) Try changing the "its" in your sentence to "his" and if it doesn't make sense, then go with "it's."

Jerry-built/Jury-Rigged

Although their etymologies are obscure and their meanings overlap, these are two distinct expressions. Something poorly built is "jerry-built." Something rigged up temporarily in a makeshift manner with materials at hand, often in an ingenious manner, is "jury-rigged." "Jerry-built" always has a negative connotation, whereas one can be impressed by the cleverness of a jury-rigged solution. Many people cross-pollinate these two expressions and mistakenly say "jerry-rigged" or "jury-built."

Jew/Jewish

"Jew" as an adjective ("Jew lawyer") is an ethnic insult; the word is "Jewish." But people who object to "Jew" as a noun are being oversensitive. Most Jews are proud to be called Jews. The expression "to Jew someone down"—an expression meaning "to Bargain for a lower price"—reflects a grossly insulting stereotype and should be avoided in all contexts.

Jewelry

Often mispronounced "joolereee." To remember the standard pronunciation, just say "jewel" and add "-ree" on the end. The British spelling is much Fancier: "jewellery."

Judgement/Judgment

In Great Britain and many of its former colonies, "judgment" is still the correct spelling; but ever since Noah Webster decreed the first E superfluous, Americans have omitted it. Many of Webster's crotchets have faded away (each year fewer people use the spelling "theater," for instance); but even the producers of terminator 2: Judgment Day, chose the traditional American spelling. If you write "judgement" you should also write "colour" and "tyre."

Kick-Start/Jump-Start

You revive a dead battery by jolting it to life with a jumper cable: an extraordinary measure used in an emergency. So if you hope to stimulate a foundering economy, you want to jump-start it. Kick-starting is just the normal way of getting a motorcycle going.

Koala Bear/Koala

A kola is not a bear. People who know their marsupials refer to them simply as "koalas."

Laissez-Faire

The mispronunciation "lazy-fare" is almost irresistible in English, but this is a French expression meaning "let it be" or, more precisely, "the economic doctrine of avoiding state regulation of the economy," and it has retained its French pronunciation (though with an English R): "lessay fare. "It is most properly used as an adjective, as in "laissez-faire capitalism, "but is also commonly used as if it were a noun phrase: "the Republican party advocates laissez-faire."

Large/Important

In colloquial speech it's perfectly normal to refer to something as a "big problem," but when people create analogous expressions in writing, the result is awkward. Don't write "this is a large issue for our firm" when what you mean is "this is an important issue for our firm." Size and intensity are not synonymous.

Last Name/Family Name

Now that few people know what a "surname" is, we usually use the term "last name" to designate a family name; but in a host of languages the family name comes first. "Julius" was the family name of Julius Caesar, and "Kawabata" was the family name of author Kawabata Yasumari. For Asians, this situation is complicated because publishers and immigrants often switch names to conform to Western practice, so you'll find most of Kawabata's books in an

American bookstore by looking under "Yasunari Kawabata." It's safer with international names to write "given name" and "family name" rather than "first name" and "last name."

Late/Former

If you want to refer to your former husband, don't call him your "late husbad" unless he's dead.

Later/Latter

Except in the expression "latter-day (modern), the word "latter" usually refers back to the last-mentioned of a set of alternatives. "We gave the kids a choice of a vacation in Paris, Rome, or Disney World. Of course the latter was their choice." In other contexts not referring back to such a list, the word you want is "later."

Lay/Lie

You lay down the book you've been reading, but you lie down when you go to bed. In the present tense, if the subject is acting on some other object, it's "lay." If the subject is lying down, then it's "lie." This distinction is often not made in informal speech, partly because in the past tense the words sound much more alike: "He lay down for a nap," but "He laid down the law." If the subject is already at rest, you night "let it lie." If a helping verb is involved, you need the past participle forms. "Lie" becomes "lain" and "lay" becomes "laid.": "He had just lain down for a nap," and "His daughter had laid the gerbil on his nose."

Leach/Leech

Water leaches chemicals out of soil or color out of cloth, your brother-in-law leeches off the family by constantly borrowing money to pay his gambling debts (he behaves like a bloodsucking leech).

Lead/led

When you're hit over the head, the instrument could be a "lead" pipe. But whenit's a verb, "lead" is the present and "led" is the past tense.

The problems is that the past tense is pronounced exactly like the above-mentioned plumbing material ("plumb" comes from a word meaning "lead"), so people confuse the two. In a sentence like "She led us to the scene of the crime," always use the three-letter spelling.

Leave/Let

The colloquial use of "leave" to mean "let" in phrases like "leave me be" is not standard. "Leave me alone" is fine, though.

Legend/Myth

Myths are generally considered to be traditional stories whose importance lies in their significance, like the myth of the Fall in Eden; whereas legends can be merely famous deeds, like the legend of Davy crockett. In common usage "myth" usually implies fantasy. Enrico Caruso was a legendary tenor, but Hogwarts is a mythical school. Legends may or may not be true. But be cautious about using "myth" to mean "untrue story" in a mythology, theology, or literature class, where teachers can be quite touchy about insisting that the true significance of a myth lies not in its factuality but in its meaning for the culture which produces or adopts it.

Lense/Lens

Although the variant spelling "lense" is listed in some dictionaries, the standard spelling for those little disks that focus light is "lens."

Liable/Libel

If you are likely to do something you are liable to do it; and if a debt can legitimately be charged to you, you are liable for it. A person who defames you with a false accusation libels you. There is no such word as "liable."

Library/Library

The first R in "library" is often slurred or omitted in speech, and it sometimes drops out in writing as well; and "librarian" is often turned into "librarian."

Light-Year

"Light-year" is always a measure of distance rather than of time; in fact it is the distance that light travels in a year. "Parsec" is also a measure of distance, equaling 3.26 light-years, though the term was used incorrectly as a measure of time by Han Solo in "Star wars."

Please, "Star wars" fans, don't bother sending me elaborate explanations of why Solo's speech makes sense; I personally heard George Lucas admit in a TV interview that it was just a mistake.

Lighted/Lit

Don't fret over the difference between these two words; they're interchangeable.

Like

Since the 1950s, when it was especially associated with hipsters, "like" as a sort of meaningless verbal hiccup has been common in speech. The earliest uses had a sort of sense to them in which "like" introduced feelings or perceptions which were then specified: "When I learned my poem had been rejected I was, like, devastated." However, "like" quickly migrated elsewhere in sentences: "I was like, just going down the road, when, like, I saw this cop, like, hiding behind the billboard," This habit has spread throughout American society, affecting people of all ages. Those who have the irritating "like" habit are usually unaware of it, even if they use it once or twice in every sentence: but if your job involves much speaking with others, it's a habit worth breaking.

Recently young people have extended its uses by using "like" to introduce thoughts and speeches: "When he tells me his car broke down on the way to my party I'm like, I now you were with Cheryl because she told me so." "To be reacted to as a grown-up, avoid this pattern. (see also "goes.")

Like/As If

"As if" is generally preferred in formal writing over "like" in sentences such as "the conductor looks as if he's ready to begin the symphony." But in colloquial speech, "like" prevails, and when recording expressions such as "he spends money like it's going out of style" it would be artificial to substitute "as if." And in expressions where the verb is implied rather than expressed, "like" is standard rather than "as": "she took to gymnastics like a duck to water."

Like for/Like

I would like you to remember that saying "I'd like for you to take out the garbage" is not formal English. The "for" is unnecessary.

"Lite" Spelling

Attempts to "reform" English spelling to render it more phonetic have mostly been doomed to failure—luckily for us. These proposed changes, if widely adopted, would make old books difficult to read and obscure etymological roots which are often a useful guide to meaning. A few, like "lite" for light," "nite" for "night" and "thru" for "through" have attained a degree of popular acceptance, but none of these should be used in formal writing. "Catalog" has become an accepted substitute for "catalogue," but I don't like it and refuse to use it. "Analog" has triumphed in technical contexts, but humanists are still more likely to write "analogue."

Literally

Like "incredible," "literally" has been so overused as a sort of vague intensifier that it is in danger of losing its literal meaning. It should be used to distinguish between a figurative and a literal meaning of a phrase. It should not be used as a synonym for "actually" or "really." Don't say of someone that he "literally blew up" unless he swallowd a stick of dynamite.

Lived

In expressions like "long-lived" pronouncing the last part to rhyme with "dived" is more traditional, but rhyming it with "sieved" is so common that it's now widely acceptable.

Lose/Loose

This confusion can easily be avoided if you pronounce the word intended aloud. If it has a voiced Z sound, then it's "lose." If it has a hissy S sound, then it's "loose." Here are examples of correct usage: "He tends to lose his key." "She lets her dog run loose." Note that when "loss" turns into "losing" it loses its "E."

Lustful/Lusty

"Lusty" means "brimming with vigor and good health" or "enthusiastic." Don't confuse it with "lustful," which means "filled with sexual desire."

Manle/Mantel

Though they stem from the same word, a "mantle" today is usually a cloak, while the shelf over a fireplace is fireplace is most often spelled "mantel."

Marital/Martial

"Marital 'refers to marriage, "martial" to war, whose ancient god was Mars. These two are often swapped, with comical results.

Marshall/Marshal

You may write "the Field Marshal marshalled his troops," but youcannot spell his title with a double "L." A marshal is always a marsha, never a marshall.

Marshmellow/Marshmallow

Your's mores may taste mellow, but that gooey confection you use in them is not "marshmallow," but "marshmallow." It was originally made from the root of a mallow plant which grew in marshes.

Mass/Massive

When the dumb coneheads on Saturday Night live talked about consuming "mass quantities" of beer they didn't know any better, but native Earth humans should stick with "massive" unless they are trying to allude to SNL. "Mass" is often used by young people in expressions where "many" or even the informal "a lot of" would be more appropriate.

Masseuse/Masseur

"Masseuse" is a strictly female term; Monsieur philippe, who gives back rubs down at the men's gym, is a masseur. Because of the unsavory associations that have gathered around the term "masseuse," serious practitioners generally prefer to be called "massage therapists."

Mauve

"Mauve" (a kind of purple) is pronounced to rhyme with "grove," not "mawv."

May/Might

Most of the time "might" and "may" are almost interchangeable, with "might" suggesting a somewhat lower probability. You're more likely to get wet if the forecaster says it may rain than if she says it might rain; but substituting one for the other is unlikely to get you into trouble—so long as you stay in the present tense.

But "might" is also the past tense of the auxiliary verb "may," and is required in sentences like "Chuck might have avoided arrest for the robbery if he hadn't given the teller his business card before asking for the money." When speculating that events might have been other than they were, don't substitute "may" for "might."

As an aside: if you are an old-fashioned child, you will ask, "May I go out to play?" rather than "can I go out to play?" Despite the prevalence of the latter pattern, some adults still feel strongly that "may" has to do with permission whereas "can" implies only physical ability. But then if you have a parent like this you've had this pattern drilled into your head long before you encountered this page.

Medal/Metal/Meddle/Mettle

A person who proves his or her mettle displays courage or stamina. The word "mettle" is seldom used outside of this expression, so people constantly confuse it with other similar-sounding words.

Media/Medium

There are several words with Latin or Greek roots whose plural forms ending in A are constantly mistaken for singular ones. See, for instance, "criteria" and "data." Radio is a broadcast medium. Television is another broadcast medium. Newspapers are a print medium. Together they are media. Following the tendency of Americans to abbreviate phrase, with "transistor radio" becoming "transistor," (now fortunately obsolete) and "videotape" becoming "video," "news media" and "communications media" have been abbreviated to "media." Remember that watercolor on paper and oil on black velvet are also media, though they have nothing to do with the news. When you want to get a message from you late Uncle fred, you may consult a medium. The word means a vehicle between some source of information and the recipient of it. The "media" are the transmitters of the news; they are not the news itself.

Medieval Ages/Middle Ages

The "eval" of "Medieval" means "age" so saying "Medieval Ages" you are saying "Middle Ages Ages." Medievalists also greatly resent the common misspelling "Midevil."

Medium/Median

That strip of grass separating the lanes going opposite directions in the middle of a freeway is a median.

Memorium/Memoriam

The correct spelling of the Latin phrase is "in memoriam."

Mic/Mike

Until very recently the casual term for a microphone was "mike," not "mic." Young people now mostly imitate the technicians who prefer the shorter "mic" label on their soundboards, but it looks distinctly odd to those used to the traditional term. There are no other words in English in which "-ic" is pronounced to rhyme with "bike"-that's the reason for the traditional "mike" spelling in the first place.

Might could/Might, could

In some American dialects it is common to say things like "I might could pick up some pizza on the way to the party." In standard English, "might" or "could" are used by themselves, not together.

Mischievious/Mischievous

The correct pronunciation of this word is "MISS-chuh-vuss," not "miss-CHEE-vee-uss." Don't let that mischievous extra "I" sneak into the word.

Moral/Morale

If you are trying to make people behave properly, you are policing their morals; if you are just trying to keep their spirits up, you are trying to maintain their morale. "Moral" is accented on the first syllable, "morale" on the second.

More Importantly/More Important

When speakers are trying to impress audiences with their rhetoric, they often seem to feel that the extra syllable in "importantly" lends weight to their remarks; "and more importantly, I have an abiding love for the American people." However, these pompous speakers are wrong. It is rarely correct to use this form of the phrase because it is seldom adverbial in intention. Say "more important" instead. The same applies to "most importantly'; it should be "most important."

Moreso/More so

"More so" should always be spelled as two distinct words.

Most Always/Almost Always

"Most always" is a casual, slangy way of saying "almost always." The latter expression is better in writing.

Motion/Move

When you make a motion in a meeting, say simply "I move," as in "I move to adjourn"; and if you're taking the minutes, write "Barbara moved," not "Barbara motioned" (unless Barbara was making wild arm-waving) gestures to summon the servers to bring in the lunch). Instead of "I want to make a motion—" It's simpler and more direct to say "I want to move—"

Much Differently/very differently

Say "we consistently vote very differently," not "much differently." But you can say "My opinion doesn't much differ from yours."

Music/Singing

After my wife—an accomplished soprano—reported indigantly that a friend of here had stated that her church had "no music, only singing," I began to notice the same tendency among my students to equate music strictly with instrumental music. I was told by one that "the singing interfered with the music" (i.e. the accompaniment). In the classical realm most listeners seem to prefer instrumental to vocal performances, which is odd given the distinct unpopularity of strictly instrumental popular music. People rejoice at the sound of choral works at Christmas but seldom seek them out at other times of the year. Serious music lovers rightly object to the linguistic sloppiness that denies the label "music" to works by such composers as Palestrina, Schubert, and Verdi. From the Middle Ages to the late eighteenth century, vocal music reigned supreme, and instrumentalists strove to achieve the prized compliment of "sounding like the human voice." The dominance of orchestral works is a comparatively recent phenomenon.

In contrast, my students often call instrumental works "songs," being unfamiliar with the terms "composition" and "piece." All singing is music, but not all music is singing.

Mute Point/Moot point

"Moot" is a very old word related to "meeting," specifically a meeting where serious matters are discussed. Oddly enough, a moot point can be a point worth discussing at a meeting (or in court)—an unresolved question—or it can be the opposite: a point already settled and not worth discussing further. At any rate, "mute point"; is simply wrong.

Myriad of/Myriad

Some traditionalists object to the word "of" after "myriad" or an "a" before, though both are fairly common in formal writing. The word is originally Greek, meaning 10,000, but now usually means "a great many." Its main function is as a noun, and the adjective derived from it shows its origins by being reluctant to behave like other nouns expressing amount, like "ton" as in "I've got a ton of work to do." In contrast: "I have myriad tasks to complete at work."

Nauseated/Nauseous

Many people say, when sick to their stomachs, that they feel "nauseous" (pronounced "NOSH-uss" or "NOZH-uss") but traditionalists insist that this word shold be used to describe something that makes you want to throw up: something nauseating. They hear you as saying that you make people want to vomit, and it tempers their sympathy for your plight. Better to say you are "nauseated," or simply that you feel like throwing up. Note that the English use "sick" exclusively for vomiting; when Americans say they feel sick, the English say they feel ill. Americans vesting Great Britain who tell their hosts they feel sick may cause them to worry needlessly about the carpeting.

Neice/Niece

Many people have trouble believing that words with the "ee" sound in them should be spelled with an "IE." The problem is that in English (and only in English), the letter I sounds like "aye" rather than "ee," as it does in the several European languages from which we have borrowed a host of words. If you had studied French in high school you would have learned that this word is pronounced "knee-YES" in that language, and it would be easier to remember. Americans in particular misspell a hos of German-Jewish names because they have trouble remembering that in that language IE is pronounced "ee" and EI is pronounced "aye." The possessors of such names are inconsistent about this matter in Enlgish. "Wein" changes from "vine" to "ween," but "klein"remains "Kline."

Next Store/Next Door

You can adore the boy next door, but not "next store."

Nieve/Naive

People who spell this French-derived word "nieve" make themselves look naïve. In French there is also a masculine form: "naif"; and both words can be nouns meaning "naive person" as well as adjectives. "Nieve" is actually the Spanish word for "snow. Naivete" is the Frenc spelling of the related noun in English.

If you prefer more nativized spelling, "naivety" is also acceptable.

Eighteen Hundreds/Nineteenth Century

"Eighteen hundreds," "sixteen hundreds" and so forth are not exactly errors; the problem is that they are used almost exclusively by people who are nervous about saying "nineteenth century" when, after all, the years in that century begin with the number eighteen. This should be simple: few people are unclear about the fact that this is the twenty-first century even though our dates being with twenty. Just be consistent about adding one to the second digit in a year and you've got the number of its century. It took a hundred years to get to the year 100, so the next hundred years, which are named "101," "102" etc. were in the second century. This also words BC. The four hundreds BC are the fifth century BC. Using phrases like "eighteen hundreds" is a signal to your readers that you are weak in math and history alike.

No sooner when/No sooner than

The phrase, "No sooner had Paula stopped petting the cat when it began to yowl" should be instead, "No sooner had Paula stopped petting the cat than it began to yowl."

Not Hardly/Not At all

"Not hardly" is slang, fine when you want to be casual—but in a formal document? Not hardly!

Noone/No one

Shall we meet at Ye Olde Sandwyche Shoppe at Noone? "No one" is always two separate words, unlike "anyone" and "someone."

Notorious

"Notorious" means famous in a bad way, as in "Nero was notorious for giving long recitals of his tedious poetry." Occasionally writers deliberately use it in a positive sense to suggest irony or wit, but this is a very feeble and tired device. Nothing admirable should be called "notorious."

Nuclear

This isn't a writing problem, but a pronunciation error. President Eisenhower used to consistently insert a "U" sound between the first and second syllables, leading many journalists to imitate him and say "nuk-yuh-lar" instead of the correct "nuk-lee-ar." The confusion extends also to "nucleus." Many people can't even hear the mistake when they make it, and only scientists and a few others will catch the mispronunciation; but you lose credibility if you are an anti-nuclear protester who doesn't know how to pronounce "nuclear." Here's one way to remember: we need a new, clear understanding of the issues; let's stop saying "Nuke you!"

Numbers

If your writing contains numbers, the general rule is to spell out in letters all the numbers from zero to nine and use numerals for larger numbers; but there are exceptions. If what you're writing is full of numbers and you're doing math with them, stick with numerals. Approximations like "about thirty days ago" and catch-phrases like "his first thousand days" are spelled out. Large round numbers are often rendered thus: "50 billion sold." With measurements, use numerals: "4 inches long." Never start a sentence with a numeral. Either spell out the number involved or rearrange the sentence to move number to a later position.

Nuptual/Nuptial

"Nuptial" is usually a pretentious substitute for "wedding," but if you're going to use it, be sure to spell it properly.

Of___'S

Phrases combining "of" with a noun followed by "S" may seem redundant, since both indicate possession; nevertheless, "a friend of Karen "s" is standard English, just as "a friend of Karen" and "Karen's friend" are.

Offense/Offence

In the US "offense" is standard; in the U.K. use "offence." The sports pronunciation accenting the first syllable should not be used when discussing military, legal, or other sorts of offense.

Often

People striving for sophistication often pronounce the "T" in this word, but true sophisticates know that the masses are correct in saying "often."

Ok/Okay

This may be the most universal word in existence; it seems to have spread to most of the world's languages. Etymologists now generally agree that it began as a humorous misspelling of "all correct": "oll korrect." "Ok" without periods is the most common form in written American English now, though "okey" is not incorrect.

Old Fashion/old-Fashioned

Although "old fashion" appears in advertising a good deal, the traditional spelling is "old–fashioned."

Old-Timer's Disease/Alzheimer's disease

I've always though that "old-timer's disease" was a clever if tasteless pun on "Alzheimer's Disease"; but many people have assured me that this is a common and quite unintentional error.

On Accident/By Accident

Although you can do things on purpose, you do them by accident.

Once and a while/once in a while

The expression is "once in a while."

One of the (Singular)

In phrases like "pistachio is one of the few flavors that appeals to me," use the singular form for the verb "appeals" because its subject is "one," not "flavors."

One-Dimensional/Two-Dimensional

Once upon a time most folks knew that "three-dimensional" characters or ideas were rounded, fleshed out, and complex and "two-dimensional" ones were flat and uninteresting. It seems that the knowledge of basic geometry has declined in recent years, because today we hear uninteresting characters and ideas described as "one-dimensional." According to Euclid, no object can be "one-dimensional (of course, accoding to modern physics, even two-dimensionality is only an abstract concept). If you are still bothered by the notion that two dimensions are one too many, just use "flat."

One In the same/One and the same

The old expression "they are one and the same" is now often mangled into the roughly phonetic equivalent "one in the same." The use of "one" here to mean "identical with each other" is familiar from phrases like "Jane and Johan act as one." They are one, they are the same.

One of the only/one of the few

"Only" has its root in "one," as should be obvious from looking at it. But we lose sight of this because of phrases like "only a few" and "only some," which lead in turn to the mistaken "one of the only." "The only" always refers to just one item, so the correct expression is "one of the few." Compare this with the similarly mistaken "very unique."

Onto/On to

"Onto" and "on to" are often interchangeable, but not always. Consider the effect created by wrongly using "onto" in the following sentence when "on to" is meant: "We're having hors d'oeuvres in the garden, and for dinner moving onto the house." If the "on" is part of an expression like "moving on" it can't be shoved together with a "to" that just happens to follow it.

Oppress/Repress

Dictators commonly oppress their citizens and repress dissent, but these words don't mean exactly the same thing. "Repress" just means "keep under control." Sometimes repression is a good thing: "During the job interview, repress the temptation to tell Mr. Brown that he has toilet paper stuck to his shoe." Oppression is always bad, and implies serious persecution.

Orders of Magnitude

Many pretentious writers have begun to use the expression "orders of magnitude" without understanding what it means. The concept derives from the scientific notation of very large numbers in which each order of magnitude is ten times the previous one. When the bacteria in a flask have multiplied from some hundreds to some thousands, it is very handy to say that their numbers have increased by an order of magnitude, and when they have increased to some millions, that their numbers have increased by four orders of magnitude.

Number language generally confuses people. Many seem to suppose that a 100% increase must be pretty much the same as an increase by an order of magnitude, but in fact such an increase represents merely a doubling of quantity. A "hundredfold increase" is even bigger: one hundred times as much. If you don't have a firm grasp on such concepts, it's best to avoid the expression altogether. After all, "our audience is ten times as big now as when the show opened" makes the same point more clearly than "Our audience has increased by an order of magnitude." compare with "quantum leap."

Ordinance/Ordnance

A law is an ordinance, but a gun is a piece of ordnance.

Oregon

Oregon natives and other westerners pronounce the state name's last syllable to sound like "gun," not "gone."

Organic

The word "organic" is used in all sorts of context, often in a highly metaphorical manner; the subject here is its use in the phrase "organic foods" in claims of superior healthfulness. Various jurisdictions have various standards for "organic" food, but generally the label is applied to foods that have been grown without artificial chemicals or pesticide. Literally, of course, the term is a redundancy: all food is composed of organic chemicals (complex chemicals containing carbon). There is no such thing as an inorganic food (unless you count water as food). Natural fertilizers and pesticides may or may not be superior to artificial ones, but the proper distinction is not between organic and inorganic. Many nitrogen-fixing plants like peas do a great job of fertilizing the soil with plain old inorganic atmospheric nitrogen.

When it comes to nutrition, people tend to generalize rashly from a narrow scientific basis. After a few preservatives were revealed to have harmful effects in some consumers, many products were proudly labeled "No preservatives!" I don't want harmful preservatives in my food, but that label suggests to me a warning: "Deteriorates quickly! May contain mold and other kinds of rot!" kinds of rot! Salt is a preservative.

Oriental/Asian

"Oriental" is generally considered old-fashioned now, and many find it offensive. "Asian" is preferred, but not "Asiatic." It's better to write the nationality involved, for example "Chinese" or "Indian," if you know it. "Asian" is often taken to mean exclusively "East Asian," which irritates South Asian and Central Asian people.

Orientate/Orient

Although some dictionaries have now begun to accept it, "orientate" was mistakenly formed from "orientation." The proper verb form is simply "orient." Similarly, "disorientated" is an error for "disoriented."

Ostensively/Ostensibly

This word, meaning "apparently," is spelled "ostensibly."

Over-exaggerated/Exaggerated

"Over-exaggerated" is a redundancy. If something is exaggerated, it's already overstressed.

Overdo/overdue

If you overdo the cocktails after work you may be overdue for your daughter's soccer game at 6:00.

Oversee/Overlook

When you oversee the preparation of dinner, you take control and manage the operation closely. But if you overlook the preparation of dinner you forget to prepare the meal entirely—better order pizza.

Palate/Palette/Pallet

Your "palate" is the roof of your mouth, and by extension, your sense of taste. A "palette" is the flat board an artist mixes paint on (or by extension, a range of colors). A "pallet" is either a bed (now rare, or a flat platform onto which goods are loaded.

Parallel/Symbol

Beginning literature students often write sentences like this: "He uses the rose as a parallel for her beauty" when they mean " a symbol for her beauty." If you are taking a literature class, it's good to master the distinctions between several related terms relating to symbolism. An Engle clutching a bundle of arrows and an olive branch is a symbol of the U.S. government in war and peace.

Students often misuse the word "analogy" in the same way. An analogy has to be specifically spelled out by the writer, not simply referred to: "My mother's attempts to find her keys in the morning were like early expeditions to the South pole: prolonged and mostly futile."

A metaphor is a kind of symbolism common in literature. When Shakespeare writes "That time of year thou mayst in me behold/When yellow leaves, or none, or few, do bang/upon those boughs which shake against the cold" he is comparing his aging self to a tree in late autumn, perhaps even specifically suggesting that he is going bald by referring to the tree shedding its leaves. This autumnal tree is a metaphor for the human aging process.

A simile resembles a metaphor except that "like" or "as" or something similar is used to make the comparison explicitly. Byron admires a dark-haired woman by saying of her "She walks in beauty, like the night/of cloudless climes and starry skies." Her darkness is said to be like that of the night.

An allegory is a symbolic narrative in which characters may stand for abstract idea, and the story convey a philosophy. Allegories are no longer popular, but the most commonly read one in school is Dante's Divine Comedy in which the poet Virgil is a symbol for human wisdom, Dante's beloved Beatrice is a symbol of divine grace, and the whole poem tries to tries to teach the reader how to avoid damnation. Aslan in C.S. Lewis' Narnia tales is an allegorical figure meant to symbolize Christ: dying to save others and rising again ("aslant" is Turkish for "lion").

Parallelled/Paralieled

In British two pairs of parallel "L'" are a handy spelling reminder, but in American English the spelling of the past tense of "parallel" is "paralleled." The same pattern holds for British "paralleling" and American "paralleling."

Parallelism in a series

Phrases in a series separated by commas or conjunctions must all have the same grammatical form. "They loved mountain-climbing, to gather wild mushrooms, and first aid practice" should be corrected to something like this: "They oved to climb mountains, gather wild mushrooms, and practice first aid" (all three verbs are dependent on that initial "to"). Fear or being repetitious often leads writers into awkward inconsistencies when creating such series.

Paralyzation/Paralysis

Some people derive the noun "paralyzation" from the verb "paralyze," but the proper term is "paralysis."

Parameters/Perimeters

When parameters were spoken of only by mathematicians and scientists, the term caused few problems; but now that it has become widely adopted by other speakers, it is constantly confused with "perimeters." A parameter is a quantity or constant that varies depending on the instance being examined. The parameters of distance between the axles of a car and its turning radius are related. The perimeter of something is its boundary. The two words shade into each other because we often speak of factors of an issue or problem being parameters, simultaneously thinking of them as limits; but this is to confuse two distinct, if related ideas. A safe rule is to avoid using "parameters" altogether unless you are confident you know what it means.

Parentheses

The most common error in using parenthesis marks (besides using them too much) is no forget to enclose the parenthetical material with a final, closing parenthesis mark. The second most common is to place concluding punctuation incorrectly. The simplest sort of example is one in which the entire sentence is enclosed in parentheses. (Most people understand that the final punctuation mush remain inside the closing parenthesis mark, like this.) More troublesome are sentences in which only a clause or phrase is enclosed in parentheses. Normally a sentence's final punctuation mark—whether period, exclamation point or qustion mark—goes outside such a parenthesis (like this). However, if the material inside the parenthesis requires a concluding punctuation mark like an exclamation point or question mark (but not a period!), that mark s placed inside the closing mark even though another mark is outside it. This latter sort of thing is awkward, however, and best avoided it you can help it.

For some reason, many writers have begun to omit the space before a parenthetic page citation, like this: (p. 17). Always preserve the space,

Parliment/Parliament

Americans unfamiliar with parliamentary systems often mistakenly leave the second "A" out of "parliament" and "parliamentary."

Passed/Past

If you are referring to time or distance, use "past": "the team performed well in the past," "the police car drove past the suspect's house." If you are referring to the action of passing, however, you need to use "passed": "When John passed the gravy, he spilled it on his lap, "the teacher was astonished that none of the students had passed the test."

Passive voice

There are legitimate uses for the passive voice: "this absurd regulation was of course written by a committee." But it's true that you can make your prose more lively and readable by using the active voice much more often. "The victim was attacked by three men in ski masks" isn't nearly as striking as "three men in ski masks attacked the victim." The passive voice is often used to avoid taking responsibility for an action: "my term paper was accidentally deleted" avoids station the truth: "I accidentally deleted my term paper." Over-use of passive constructions is irritating, though not necessarily erroneous. But it does lead to real clumsiness when passive constructions get piled on top of each other: "no exception in the no-pets rule was sought to be crated so that angora rabbits could be raised in the apartment" can be made clear by shifting to the active voice: "the landlord refused to make an exception to the no-pets rule to allow Eliza to raise angora rabbits in the apartment.

Past Time/Pastime

An agreeable activity like knitting with which you pass the time is your pastime. Spell it as one word, with one "S" and one "T".

Pawn off /Palm off

Somebody defrauds you by using sleight of hand (literal or figurative) to "palm" the object you wanted and give you something inferior) instead. The expression is not "to pawn off," but "to palm off."

Peace/Piece

It's hard to believe many people really confuse the meaning of these words; but the spellings are frequently swapped, probably out of sheer carelessness. "Piece" has the word "pie" buried in it, which should remind you of the familiar phrase, "a piece of pie." You can meditate to find peace of mind, or you can get angry and give someone a piece of your mind. Classical scholars will note that "pox" is the Latin word for peace, suggesting the need for an "A" in the latter word.

Peak/Peek/Pique

It is tempting to think that your attention night be aroused to a high point by "peaking" your curiosity; but in fact, "pique" is a French word meaning "Prick," in the sense of "stimulate." The expression has nothing to do with "peek," either." Therefore the expression is "my curiosity was piqued."

Peasant/Pheasant

When I visited the former Soviet Union I was astonished to learn that farm workers were still called "peasants" there. In English-speaking countries we tend to think of the term as belonging strictly to the feudal era. However you use it, don't confuse it with "pheasant," a favorite game bird. Use the sound of the beginning consonants to remind you of the difference: pheasants are food, peasants are people.

Penultimate/Next to Last

To confuse your readers, use the term "penultimate," which means "next to last," but which most people assume means "the very last." And if you really want to baffle them, use "antepenultimate" to mean "third from the end."

Many people also mistakenly use "penultimate" when they mean "quintessential" or "archetypical."

Per/According to

Using "per" to mean "according to" as in "ship the widgets as per the instructions of the customer" is rather old-fashioned business jargon, and is not welcome in other contexts. "Per" is fine when used in phrases involving figures like "miles per gallon."

Pernickety/Persnickety

The original Scottish dialect from was "pernickety," but Americans changed it to "persnickety" a century ago. "Pernickety" is generally unknown in the U.S. though it's still in wide use across the Atlantic.

Perogative/ Prerogative

"Prerogative" is frequently both mispronounced and misspelled as "preogative." It may help to remember that the word is associated with PRivileges of PRecedence.

Perpetuate/Perpetrate

"Perpetrate" is something criminals do (criminals are sometimes called "preps" in cop slang). When you seek to continue something you are trying to perpetuate it.

Perse/Per Se

This legal term meaning "in, of, or by itself" is a bit pretentious, but you gain little respect if you misspell per se as a single word. Worse is the mistaken "per say."

Personal/Personal

Employees are personnel, but private individuals considered separately from their jobs have personal lives.

Perspective/Prospective

"Perspective" has to do with sight, as in painting, and is usually a noun. "Prospective" generally has to do with the future (compare with "what are your prospects, young man?") and is usually an adjective. But beware: there is also a rather old-fashioned but fairly common meaning of the word "prospect" that has to do with sight: "as he climbed the mountain, a vast prospect opened up before him."

Persecute/Prosecute

When you persecute someone, you're treating them badly, whether they deserve it or not; but only legal officers can prosecute someone for a crime.

Peruse

This word, which means "examine thoroughly" is often misused to mean "glance over hastily." Although some dictionaries accept the latter meaning, it is not traditional.

Phenomena/Phenomenon

There are several words with Latin or Greek roots whose plural forms ending in "A" are constantly mistaken for singular ones. See, for instance, "criteria" and "media" and "data." It's "this phenomenon," but "these phenomena."

Philippines/Filipinos

The people of the Philippines are called "Filipinos." Don't switch the initial letters of these two words.

Physical/Fiscal

In budget matters, It's the fiscal year, relating finances with an "F."

Picaresque/Picturesque

"Picaresque" is a technical literary term you are unlikely to have a use for. It labels as sort of literature involving a picaro (Spanish), a lovable rogue who roams the land having colorful adventures. A landscape that looks as lovely as a picture is picturesque.

Picture

The pronunciation of "picture" as if it were "pitcher" is common some dialects, but not standard. The first syllable should sound like "pick."

Pin number/Pin

Those who object to "PIN number" on the grounds that the N in "PIN" stands for "numbr" in the phrase "personal identification number" are quite right, but it may be difficult to get people to say anything else.

"PIN" was invented to meet the objection that a "password" consisting of nothing but numbers is not a word. Pronouncing each letter of the acronym as "P-I-N" blunts its efficiency. Saying just "PIN' reminds us of another common English words though few people are likely to think when they are told to "enter PIN" that they should shove a steel pin into the terminal they are operating. In writing, anyway, PIN is unambiguous and should be used without the redundant "number."

The same goes for "VIN number"; "VIN" stands for "Vehicle Identification. Number." And "UPC code" is redundant because "UPC" stands for "Universal Product Code."

Playwrite/Playwright

It might seem as if a person who writes plays should be called a "playwright"; but in fact a playwright is a person who has wrought wheels out of wood and iron. All the other words ending in "-Wright" are archaic, or we'd be constantly reminded of the correct pattern.

Plead Innocent

Lawyers frown on the phrase plead innocent" (it's "plead guilty" or "plead not guilty"); but outside of legal contexts the phrase is standard English.

Please RSVP/Please Reply

R.S.V.P. stands for the French phrase "Repondez s'il vos plait" ("reply, please"), so it doesn't need an added "please." However, since few people seem to know its literal meaning, and fewer still take it seriously, it's best to use plain English: "please reply." And for those of you receiving such an invitation: yes, you have to let the host know whether you're coming or not, and no, you can't bring along the kids or other uninvited guests.

Plug-In/Outlet

That thing on the end of an electrical cord is a plug, which goes into the socket of the wall outlet.

Point Being is that

"The point being is that" is redundant; say just "the point is that" or "the point being that."

Podium/Lectern

Strictly speaking, a podium is a raised platform on which you stand to give a speech; the piece of furniture on which you place your notes and behind which you stand is a lectern.

Pole/Poll

A pole is a long stick. You could take a "poll" (survey or ballot) to determine whether voters want lower taxes or better education.

Pompom/Pompon

To most people that fuzzy all on the top of a knit hat and the implement wielded by a cheerleader are both "pompoms," but to traditionalists they are "pompons," spelled the way the French—who gave us the word—spell it. A pompom, say these purists, is only a sort of large gun. Though you're unlikely to bother many people by falling into the common confusion, you can show off your education by observing the distinction.

Populace/populous

The population of a country may be referred to as its populace, but a crowded country is populous.

Pore/Pour

When used as a verb, "pore" has the unusual sense of "scrutinize," as in "She pored over her recipts." If its's coffee or rain, the stuff pours.

Possessed of/Possessed by/Possessed with

If you own a yacht, you're possessed of it. If a demon takes over your body, you're possessed by it. If that which possesses you is more metaphorical, like an executive determined to get ahead, he or she can be possessed by or with the desire to win.

Practice/Practise

In the United Kindom, "practice" is the noun, "practice" the verb; but in the U.S. the spelling "practice' is commonly used for both, though the distinction is sometimes observed. "Practice" as a noun is, however, always wrong in both places: a doctor always has a "practice," never a "practise."

Practicle/Practical

Some words end in "-icle" and others in "-ical" without the result being any difference in pronunciation. But when you want somebody really practically, call on good old AL.

Pray/prey

If you want a miracle, pray to god. If you're a criminal, you prey on your victims. Incidentally, it's "praying mantis," not "preying mantis." The insect holds its forefeet in a position suggesting prayer.

Precede/Proceed

"Precede" means" to go before." "Proceed" means to go on. Let your companion precede you through the door, then proceed to follow her. Interestingly, the second E is missing in "procedure."

Precedence/Precedents

Although these words sound the same, they work differently. The pop star is given precedence over the factory worker at the entrance to the dance club. "precedents" is just the plural of "precedent": "If we let the kids adopt that rattlesnake as a pet and agree to let them take it for a walk in death valley, we'll be setting some bad precedents."

Precipitate/Precipitious

Both of these adjectives are based on the image of plunging over the brink of a precipice, but "precipitate" emphasizes the suddenness of the plunge, "precipitous," the steepness of it. If you make a "precipitate" decision, you are making a hasty and probably unwise one. If the stock market declines "precipitously," it goes down sharply.

Predominate/Predominant

"Predominate" is a verb: "In the royal throne room, the color red predominates." " Predominant" is an adjective: "The predominant view among the touts is that Fancy Dancer is the best bet in the third race."

Predominately/Predominantly

"Predominantly" is formed on the adjective "predominant," not the verb "Predominate."

Preemptory/Peremptory

"Peremptory" (meaning "imperative") is often misspelled and mispronounced "preemptory" through confusion caused by the influence of the verb "prempt," whose adjectival form is actually "preemptive." "Preemptory" exists only as an obscure legal term you're not likely to have use for.

Prejudice/Prejudiced

People not only misspell "prejudice" in a number of ways, they sometimes say "he's prejudice" when they mean "he's prejudiced."

Premier/Premiere

These words are, respectively, the masculine and feminine forms of the word for "first" in French; but they have become differentiated in English. Only the masculine form is used as an adjective, as in "Tidy-pool is the premier pool-cleaning firm in Orange Country." The confusion arises when these words are used as nouns. The prime minister of a parliamentary government is known as a "premier." The opening night of a film or play is its "premiers." "Premiere" as a verb is common in the arts and in show business ("the show premiered on PBS"), but it is less acceptable in other contexts ("the state government premiered its new welfare system"). Use "introduced," or, if real innovation is involved, "pioneered."

Premise/Premises

Some people suppose that since "premises" has a plural form, a single house or other piece of property must be a "premise," but that word is reserved for use as a term in logic weaning something assumed or taken as given in making an argument. Your lowly one-room shack is still your premises.

Prepositions (Repeated)

In the sentence "Alex liked Nancy, with whom he shared his Snickers bar with" only one "with" is needed–eliminate either one. Look out for similarly duplicated prepositions.

Incidentally, an often–cited example of this pattern is from Paul McCartney's "Live and Let Die": "In this ever-changing world in which we live in"; but if you listen closely, you'll hear instead a quite correct. "In this ever-changing world in which we're living". "Americans have a hard time hearing the soft British "R" in "we're."

Prepositions (Wrong)

One of the clearest indications that a person reads little and doesn't hear much formal English is a failure to use the right. preposition in a common expression. You aren't ignorant to a fact; you're ignorant of it.

Things don't happen on accident, but by accident (though they do happen "on purpose"). There are no simple rules governing Preposition usage: you just have to immerse yourself in good English in order to write it naturally.

Prescribe/Proscribe

You recommend something when you prescribe it, but you forbid it when you proscribe it. The usually positive function of "pro-" confuses many people.

Presently/Currently

Some argue that "presently" doesn't mean "in the present." It means "soon." If you want to talk about something that's happening right now, they urge you to say it's going on currently.

Pretty/somewhat

It's pretty common to use "pretty" to mean "somewhat" in ordinary speech; but it should be avoided in formal writing, where sometimes "very" is more appropriate. The temptation to use "pretty" usually indicates the writer is being vague, so changing to something more specific may be an even better solution: "a pretty bad mess" might be "chocolate syrup spilled all over the pizza which had been dumped upside down on the carpet."

Primer

When this word is used in the U.S. to mean "elementary textbook" it is pronounced with a short "I": "primer" (rhymes with "dinner"). All other meanings are pronounced with along "I": "prymer" (rhymes with "timer").

Principal/principle

Generations of teachers have tried to drill this one into students' heads by reminding them, "The principal is your pal." Many don't seem convinced. "Principal" is a noun and adjective referring to someone or something which is highest in rank or importance. (In a loan, the principal is the more substantial part of the money, the interest is – or should be – the lesser.) "Principal" is only a noun, and has to do with law or doctrine: "The workers fought hard for the principle of collective bargaining."

Prioritize

Many people disdain "prioritize" as bureaucratic jargon for "rank" or "make a high priority."

Priority

It is common to proclaim "in our business, customer service is a priority," but it would be better to say "a high priority," since priorities can also be low.

Probably

The two Bs in this word are particularly difficult t pronounce in sequence, so the word often comes out as "probly" and is even occasionally misspelled that way. When even the last B disappears, the pronunciation "prolly" suggests drunken slurring or, at best, an attempt at humor.

As time progressed/as time passed

Events may progress in time, but time itself does not progress – it just passes.

Prone/supine

"Prone" (face down) is often confused with "supine" (face up). "Prostrate" technically also means "face down," but is most often used to mean simply "devastated."

Prophecy/prophesy

"Prophecy," the noun, (pronounced "PROF-a-see") is a prediction. The verb "to prophesy" (pronounced "PROF-a-sigh") means to predict something. When a prophet prophesies he or she utters prophecies.

Pronunciation/pronunciation

"Pronounce" is the verb, but the "O" is omitted for the noun: "pronunciation." This mistake ranks right up there incongruity with "writing."

Prostate/prostrate

The gland men have is called the prostate. "Prostrate" is an adjective meaning "lying face downward."

Protray/portray

There are a lot of words in English that begin in "pro-." This is not one of them. When you make a portrait, you portray someone.

Proved/Proven

For most purposes either form is a fine past participle of "prove," though in a phrase like "a proven talent" where the word is an adjective preceding a noun, "proven" is standard.

Purposely/purposefully

If you do something on purpose (not by accident), you do it purposely. But if you have a specific purpose in mind, you are acting purposefully.

Quantum leap

The thing about quantum leaps is that they mark an abrupt change from one state to a distinctly different one, with no in-between transitional states being possible; but they are not large. In fact, in physics a quantum leap is one of smallest sorts of changes worth talking about. Leave "quantum leap" to the subatomic physicists unless you know what you're talking about.

Queue

If you're standing in a queue you'll have plenty of time to ponder the unusual spelling of this word. Remember, it contains two "U" s.

Quiet/quite

This is probably caused by a slip of the fingers more often than by a slip of the mental gears, but one often sees "quite" (very) substituted for "quiet" (shhh!). This is one of those common errors your spelling checker will not catch, so look out for it.

Quote

A passage doesn't become a quote (or—better—"quotation") until you've quoted it. The only time to refer to a "quote" is when you are referring to someone quoting something. When referring to the original words, simply call it a passage.

Quotation marks

The examples below are set off in order to avoid confusion over the use of single and double quotation marks.

There are many ways to go wrong with quotation marks. They are often used ironically:

She ran around with a bunch of "intellectuals."

The quotation marks around "intellectuals" indicate that the writer believes that these are in fact so-called intellectuals, not real intellectuals at all. The ironic use of quotation marks is very much overdone, and is usually a sign of laziness indicating that the writer has not bothered to find the precise word or expression necessary.

Advertisers unfortunately tend to use quotation marks merely for emphasis.

Racism

The "C" in "racism" and "racist" is pronounced as a simple "S" sound, Don't confuse it with the "SH" sound in "racial."

Rack/Wrack

If you are racked with pain or you fell nerve-racked, you are feeling as if you were being stretched on that Medieval instrument of torture, the rack. You rack your brains when your stretch them vigorously to search out the truth like a torturer. "Wrack" has to do with ruinous accidents, so if the stock market is wracked by rumours of immient recession, it's wrecked.

Ran/run

Computer programmers have been heard to say "the program's been ran," when what they mean is "the program's been run.

Ratio

A ratio is a way of expressing the relationship between one number and another. If there is one teacher to fifty students, the teacher/student ratio is one to fifty, and the student/teacher ratio fifty to one. If a very dense but wealthy prince were being tutored by fifty teachers, the teacher/student ratio would be fifty to one, and the student/teacher ratio would be one to fifty as you can see, the order in which the numbers are compared is important.

The ratios discussed so far are "high" – the difference between the numbers is large. The lowest possible ratio is one to one: one teacher to one student. If you are campaigning for more individual attention in the classroom, you want a higher number of teachers, but a lower student/teacher ratio.

Rationale/rationalization

When you're explaining the reasoning behind your position, you're presenting your rationale. But if you're just making up some lame excuse to make your position appear better—whether to yourself or others—you're engaging in rationalization.

Ravaging/Ravishing/Ravenous

To ravage is to pillage, sack, or devastate. The only time "ravaging" is properly used is in phrases like "when the pirates had finished ravaging the town, they turned to ravishing the women." Which brings us to "ravish": meaning to rape, or rob violently. A trailer court can be ravaged by a storm (nothing is stolen, but a lot of damage is done) but not ravished. The crown jewels of Ruritania can be ravished (stolen using violence) without being ravaged (damaged).

To confuse matters, people began back in the fourteenth century to speak metaphorically of their souls being "ravished" by intense spiritual o esthetic experiences. Thus we speak of a "ravishing woman" (the term is rarely applied to men) today not because she literally rapes men who look at her but because her devastating beauty penetrates their hearts in an almost violent fashion. Despite contemporary society's heightened sensitivity about rape, we still remain (perhaps fortunately) unconscious of many of the transformations of the root meaning in words with positive connotations such as "rapturous."

Originally, "raven" as a verb was synonymous with "ravish" in the sense of "to steal by force." One of its specialized meanings became "devour," as in "the lion ravened her prey." By analogy, hungry people became "ravenous" (as hungry as beasts), and that remains the only common use of the word today.

If a woman smashes your apartment up, she ravages it. If she looks stunningly beautiful, she is ravishing. If she eats the whole platter of hors d'oeuvres you've set out for the party before the other guests come she's ravenous.

Reactionary/Reactive

Many people incorrectly use "reactionary" to mean "acting in response to some outside stimulus." "That's "reactive." "Reactionary" actually has a very narrow meaning; it is a noun or adjective describing a form of looking backward that goes beyond conservatism (wanting to prevent change and maintain present conditions) to reaction – wanting to recreate a lost past. The advocates of restoring Czarist rule in Russia are reactionaries. While we're on the subject, the term "proactive" formed by analogy with "reactive" seems superfluous to many of us. Use "active," "assertive," or "positive" whenever you can instead.

Real/really

The correct adverbial form is "really" rather than "real"; but even that form is generally confined to casual speech, as in "When you complimented me on my speech I felt really great!" To say "real great" instead moves the speaker several steps downscale socially. However "really" is a feeble qualifier. "wonderful" is an acceptable substitute for "really great" and you can give a definite upscale slant to your speech by adopting the British "really quite wonderful." Usually, however, it is better to replace the expression altogether with something more precise: "almost seven feet tall" is better than "really tall." To strive for intensity by repeating "really" as in "that dessert you made was really, really good" demonstrates an impoverished vocabulary.

Reason because

We often hear people say things like, "the reason there's a hole in the screen door is because I tripped over the cat on my way out." The phrase "is because" should be "is that." If you wanted to use "because," the sentence should be phrased, "There's a hole in the screen door because I tripped over the cat." Using both is a redundancy, as it the common expression "the reason why." "The reason being is" should be simply "the reason being."

Rebelling/revolting

Even though "rebel" and "revolt" mean more or less the same thing, people who are revolting are disgusting, not taking up arms against the government.

Rebut/refute

When you rebut someone's argument you argue against it. To refute someone's argument is to prove it incorrect. Unless you are certain you have achieved success, use "rebut."

Recent/resent

There are actually three words to distinguish here. "Recent," always pronounced with an unvoiced hissy S and with the accent on the first syllable, means "not long ago," as in, "I appreciated your recent encouragement." "Resent" has two different meanings with two different pronunciations, both with the accent on the second syllable. In the most common case, where "recent" means "feel bad about," the word is pronounced with a voiced Z sound: "I resent your implication that I gave you the chocolates only because I was hoping you'd share them with me." In the less common case, the word means "to send again," an is pronounced with an unvoiced hissy S sound: "The e-mail message bounced, so I resent it." So say the intended word aloud. If the accent is on the second syllable, "recent' is the spelling you need.

Recreate/reinvent

The expression "no need to reinvent the wheel" loses much of its wit when "recreate" is substituted for the original verb. While we're at it, "recreate' does not mean "to engage in recreation." If you play basketball, you may be exercising, but you're not recreating.

Recuperate/recoup

If you are getting over an illness, you are recuperating; but if you insist on remaining at the roulette table when your luck has been running against you, you are seeking to recoup your losses.

Reeking havoc/wreaking havoc

"Reeking" means "smelling strongly," so that can't be right. The phrase simply means 'working great destruction." "Havoc" has always referred to general destruction in English, but one very old phrase incorporating the word was "cry havoc," which meant to give an army to signal for pillage. To "play havoc with" means the same thing as to "wreak havoc." Avoid as well the mistaken "wreck havoc."

Regard/regards

Business English is deadly enough without scrambling it. "As regards your downsizing plan ..." is acceptable, if stiff. "In regard to" and "with regard to" are also correct. But "in regards to" is nonstandard. You can also convey the same idea with "in respect to" or "with respect to."

Regretfully/regrettably

Either word can be used as an adverb to introduce an expression of regret, though conservatives prefer "regrettably" in sentences like "Regrettably, it rained on the 4th of July." Within the body of a sentence, however, "regretfully" may be used only to describe the manner in which someone does something: "John had to regretfully decline his beloved's invitation to go hang-gliding because he was terrified of heights." If no specified person in the sentence is doing the regretting, but the speaker is imply asserting "it is to be regretted," the word is "regrettably": "Their boss is regrettably stubborn."

Reign/rein

A king or queen reigns, but you rein in a horse. The expression "to give rein" means to give in to an impulse as a spirited horse gives in to its impulse to gallop when you slacken the reins. Similarly, the correct expression is "free rein," not "free reign."

Religion believes/religion teaches

People often write things like "Buddhism believes" when they mean to say "Buddhism teaches," or "Buddhists believe." Religions do not believe, they are the objects of belief.

Reluctant/reticent

"Reticent" denotes only reluctance to speak; do not use it for any other form of reluctance.

Remotely close

"Not even remotely close" is a fine example of an oxymoron. An idea can be "not even remotely correct," but closeness and remoteness are opposites; it doesn't make sense to have one modify the other. These are lots of lists of oxymorons on the Web, but they mostly mix jokey editorializing ("military intelligence" and "Microsoft Works") with true oxymorons. Good for a laugh, but not providing much guidance to writers.

If there's a truly helpful oxymoron site you know of I"d like to hear about it.

Remuneration/remuneration

Although "remuneration" looks as if it might mean "repayment" it usually means simply "payment." In speech it is often confused with "remuneration," re-counting (counting again).

Reoccurring/recurring

It might seem logical to form this word from "occurring" by simply adding a RE-prefix—logical, but wrong. The word is "recurring." The root form is "recur," not "reoccur." For some reason "recurrent" is seldom transformed into "reoccurrent."

Repel/repulse

In most of their meanings these are synonyms, but if you are disgusted by someone, you are repelled, not repulsed. The confusion is compounded by the fact that "repellent" and "repulsive" mean the same thing. Go figure.

Resister/resistor

A resistor is part of an electrical circuit; a person who resists something is a "resister."

Retch/wretch

If you vomit, you retch; if you behave in a wretched manner or fall into wretched circumstances, you are a wretch.

Return back/return

"Return back" is a redundancy. Use just "return," unless you mean to say instead "turn back."

Revelant/relevant

"Revelant" is both spoken and written frequently when "relevant" is intended.

Revue/review

You can attend a musical revue in a theatre, but when you write up your reactions for a newspaper, you're writing a review.

Right of passage/rite of passage

The more common phrase is "rite of passage" – a ritual one goes through to move on to the next stage of life. Learning how to work the combination on a locker is a rite of passage for many entering middle school students. A "right of passage" would be the right to travel through a certain territory, but you are unlikely to have any use for the phrase.

Rio grande river/Rio grande

Rio is the Spanish for "river," so "Rio Grande River" is a redundancy. Just write "Rio Grande." Non-Hispanic Americans have traditionally failed to pronounce the final "E" in Grande", but they've learned to do it to designate the large size of latte, so perhaps it's time to start saying it the proper Spanish way "REE-oh GRAHN-day." Or to be really international we could switch to the Mexican name: "Rio Bravo."

Risky/risque

People unfamiliar with the Fresh-derived word "risque" ("slightly indecent") often write "risky" by mistake. Bungee-jumping is risky, but nude bungee-jumping is risque.

Road to hoe/row to hoe

Out in the cotton you have a tough row to hoe. This saying has nothing to do with road construction.

Role/roll

An actor plays a role. Bill gates is the entrepreneur's role model. But you eat a sausage on a roll and roll out the barrel.

Root/rout/route

You can root for your team (cheer them on) and hope that they utterly smash their opponents (create a rout), then come back in triumph on Route 27 (a road).

Sacred/scared

This is one of those typos which your spelling checker won't catch: gods are sacred, the damned in Hell are scared.

Sacrilegious/sacreligious

Doing something sacrilegious involves committing sacrilege. Don't let the related word "religious" trick you into misspelling the word as "sacreligious."

Safety Deposit Box/Safe-Deposit Box

"Safety" is rarely pronounced very differently from "safe-D" so it is natural that many people suppose they are hearing the word at the beginning of this phrase, but the correct expression is in fact "safe-deposit box."

Sail/sale/sell

These simple and familiar words are surprisingly often confused in writing. You sail a boat which has a sail of canvas. You sell your old fondue pot at a yard sale.

Salsa sauce/salsa

"Salsa" is Spanish for "sauce," so "salsa sauce" is redundant. Here in the U.S., where people now spend more on salsa than on ketchup (or catsup, if you prefer), few people are unaware that it's a sauce. Anyone so sheltered as not to be aware of that fact will need a fuller explanation: "chopped tomatoes, onions, chilies and cilantro."

Sarcastic/ironic

Not all ironic comments are sarcastic. Sarcasm is meant to mock or wound. Irony can be amusing without being maliciously aimed at hurting anyone.

Saw/seen

In standard English, it's "I've seen" not "I've saw." The helping verb "have" (abbreviated here to "'ve") requires "seen." In the simple past (no helping verb), the expression I "I saw," not "I seen." "I've seen a lot of ugly cars, but when I saw that old beat-up Rambler I couldn't been believe my eyes."

Say/tell

You say "Hello, Mr. Chips" to the teacher, and then tell him about what you did last summer. You can't "tell that" except in expressions like "go tell that to your old girlfriend."

Schizophrenic

In popular usage, "schizophrenic" (and the more slangy and now dated "schizoid") indicates "split between two attitudes." This drives people with training in psychiatry crazy. "Schizo-" does indeed mean "split," but it is used here to mean "split off from reality." Someone with a Jekyll-and-Hyde personality is suffering from "multiple personality disorder" (or, more recently, "dissociative identity disorder"), not "schizophrenia."

Sci-fi

"Sci-fi," the widely used abbreviation for "science fiction," is objectionable to most professional science fiction writers, scholars, and many fans. Some of them scornfully designate alien monster movies and other trivial entertainments "sci-fi" (which they pronounce "skiffy") to distinguish them from true science fiction. The preferred abbreviation in these circles is "SF." The problem with this abbreviation is that to the general public "SF" means "San Francisco." "The Sci-fi channel" has exacerbated the conflict over this term. If you are a reporter approaching a science fiction writer or expert you immediately mark yourself as an outsider by using the term "sci-fi."

Seam/seem

"Seem" is the verb, "seam" the noun. Use "seam" only for things like the line produced when two pieces of cloth are sewn together or a thread of coal in a geological formation.

Second of all/second

"First of all" makes sense when you want to emphasize the primacy of the first item in a series, but it should not be followed by "second of all," where the expression serves no such function. And "secondly" is an adverbial form that makes no sense at all in enumeration (neither does "firstly"). As you go through you list, say simply "second," "third," "fourth," etc.

Select/Selected

"Select" means "special, chosen because of its outstanding qualities." If you are writing an ad for a furniture store offering low prices on some of its recliners, call them "selected recliners," not "select recliners," unless they are truly outstanding and not just leftovers you're trying to move out of the store.

Self-worth/self-esteem

To say that a person has a low sense of self-worth makes sense, though it's inelegant; but people commonly truncate the phrase, saying instead, "He has low self-worth." This would literally mean that he isn't worth much rather than that he has a low opinion of himself. "Self-esteem" sounds much more literate.

Sense/since

"Senseual" is a verb meaning "feel" ("I sense you near me") or a noun meaning "intelligence" ("have some common sense!"). Don't use it when you need the adverb "since" ("since you went away," "since you're up anyway, would you please let the cat out?")

Sensual/sensuous

"Sense" usually relates to physical desires and experiences, and often means "sexy." But "Sensuous" is more often used for esthetic pleasures, like "sensuous music." The two words do overlap a good deal. The leather seats in your new car may be sensuous; but if they turn you on, they might be sensual. "Sensual" often has a slightly racy or even judgmental tone lacking in "sensuous."

Service/serve

A mechanic services your car and a stallion services a mare; but most of the time when you want to talk about the goods or services you supply, the word you want is "serve": "Our firm serves the hotel industry."

Set/Sit

In some dialects people say "come on in and set a spell," but in standard English the word is "sit." You set down an object or a child you happen to be carrying; but those seating themselves sit.

Setup/set up

Technical writers sometimes confuse "setup" as a noun ("check the setup") with the phrase "set up" ("set up the experiment").

Shall/Will

"Will" has almost entirely replaced "shall" in American English except in legal document sand in questions like "shall we have red wine with the duck?"

Sherbert/Sherbet

The name for these icy desserts is derived from Turkish/ Persian "sorbet," but the "R" in the firt syllable seems to seduce many speakers into adding one in the second, where it doesn't belong. A California chain called "Herbert's sherbets" had me confused on this point for years when I was growing up.

Sierra Nevada Mountains/Sierra Nevadas

Sierra is Spanish for "'mountain rage," so knowledgeable westerners usually avoid a redundancy by simply referring to "the Sierra Nevadas" or simply "the Sierras." Transplanted weather forecasters often get this wrong.

Some object to the familiar abbreviation "sierras," but this form, like "Rockies" and "Smokies" too well established to be considered erroneous.

Silicon/Silicone

Silicon is a chemical element, the basic stuff of which microchips are made. Sand is largely silicon. Silicones are plastics and other materials containing silicon, the most commonly discussed example being silicone breast implants. Less used by the general public is "silica": the oxide of silicon.

Slight of Hand/Sleight of Hand

"Sleight' is old word meaning "cleverness, skill," and the proper expression is "sleight of hand." It's easy to understand why it's confused with "slight" since the two words are pronounced in exactly the same way.

Stuff off/Slough off

You use a loofah to slough off dead skin.

Snuck/Sneaked

When Huckleberry Finn "snuck" out of a house he was acting according to his character—and dialect. This is one of many cases in which people" s humorously self-conscious use of dialect has influenced others to adopt it as standard and it is now often seen even in sophisticated writing in the U.S. But it is safer to use the traditional form: "sneaked."

Sometime/Some time

"Let's get together sometime." When you use the one word form, it suggests some indefinite time in the future. "Some time" is not wrong in this sort of context, but it is required when being more specific:

"Choose some time that fits in your schedule." "Some" is an adjective here modifying "time." The same pattern applied to "someday" (vague) and "some day" (specific).

So/Very

Originally people said things like "I was so delighted with the wrapping that I couldn't bring myself to open the package." But then they began to lazily say "You made me so happy," no longer explaining just how happy that was. This pattern of using "so" as a simple intensifier meaning "very" is now standard in casual speech, but is out of place in formal writing, where "very" or another intensifier words better. Without vocal emphasis, the "so" conveys little in print.

So Fun/So Much fun

Strictly a young person's usage: "That party was so fun!" If you don't want to be perceived as a gum-chewing airhead, say "so much fun."

Social/Societal

"Societal" as an adjective has been existence for a couple of centuries, but has become widely used only in the recent past. People who imagine that "social" has too many frivolous connotations of mere partying often resort to it to make their language more serious and impressive. It is best used by social scientists and other in referring to the influence of societies: "societal patterns among the Ibo of western Nigeria." Used in place of "social" in ordinary speech and writing it sounds pretentious.

Sojourn/Journey

Although the spelling of this word confuses many people into thinking it means "journey," a sojourn is actually a temporary stay in one place. If you're constantly on the move, you're not engaged in a sojourn.

Somewhat of A/Somewhat, something of A

This error is the result of confusing two perfectly good usages: "She is somewhat awkward," and "He is something of a klutz." Use one or the other instead.

Sooner/Rather

"I'd sooner starve than eat what they serve in the cafeteria" is less formal than "I'd rather starve."

Soup Du Jour of the day/Soup of the Day

"Soupe du jour" (note the "E" on the end of "soupe") means "soup of the day." If you're going to use French to be pretentious on a menu, it's important to learn the meaning of the words you're using. Often what is offered is potage, anyway. Keep it simple, keep it in English, and you can't go wrong.

Spaded/Spayed

If you have neutered your dog, you've spayed it; save the spading until it dies.

States/Countries

Citizens of the United States, where states are smaller subdivisions of the country, are sometimes surprises to see "states' referring instead to foreign countries. Note that the U.S. Department of State deals with foreign affairs, not those of U.S. states. Clearly distinguish these two uses of "State" in your writing.

Stationary/Stationery

When something is standing still, it's stationary. That piece of paper you write a letter on is stationery.

Stomp/Stamp

"Stomp" is colloquial, casual. A professional wrestler stomps his opponent. In more formal contexts "stamp" is preferred. But you will probably not be able to stamp out the spread of "stomp."

Straightjacket/Straitjacket

The old word "strait" ("narrow, tight") has survived only as a noun in geography referring to a narrow body of water ("the Bering Strait") and in a few adjectival uses such as "straitjacket" (a narrowly confining garment) and "strait-laced" (literally laced up tightly, but usually meaning narrow-minded). Its unfamiliarity causes many people to mistakenly substitute the more common "straight."

Substance-free

An administrator at our university announced recently that his goal was a "substance-free" campus, which I suppose fits in with the growing fad of "virtual education." What he really meant was, of course, a campus free of illegal drugs and alcohol, designated "controlled substances" in the law. This is a very silly expression, but if he'd just said "sober and straight" he would have sounded too censorious. How about "drug and alcohol-free"?

Substitute with/Substitute for

You can substitute pecans for the walnuts in a brownie recipe, but many people mistakenly say "substitute with" instead, perhaps influenced by the related expression "replace with." It's always "substitute for."

Suffer with/Suffer from

Although technical medical usage sometimes differs, in normal speech we say that a person suffers from a disease rather than suffering with it.

Suit/Suite

Your bedroom suite consists of the bed, the nightstand, and whatever other furniture goes with it. Your pajamas would be your bedroom suit.

Summary/Summery

When the weather is warm and summery and you don't feel like spending a lot of time reading that long report from the restructuring committee, just read the summary.

Supercede/Supersede

"Supersede," meaning to replace, originally meant "to sit higher" than, from Latin sedere, "to sit." In the 18th century, rich people were often carried about as they sat in sedan chairs.Don't be misled by the fact that this word rhymes with words having quite different roots, such as "intercede."

Supposably or Supposingly/Supposedly

"Supposedly" is the standard form. "Supposably" can be used only when the meaning is "capable of being supposed," and then only in the U.S. you won't get into trouble if you stick with "Supposedly."

Suppose to/Supposed to

Because the D and the T are blended into a single consonant when this phrase is pronounced, many writers are unaware that the D is even present and omit it in writing. You're supposed to get this one right if you want to earn the respect of your readers. See also "use to."

Surfing the internet

"Channel-surfing" developed as an ironic term to denote the very unauthentic activity of randomly changing channels on a television set with a remote control. Its only similarity to surfboarding on real surf has to do with the esthetic of "going with the flow." The internet could be a fearsomely difficult place to navigate until the World Wide Web was invented; casual clicking on web links was naturally quickly compared to channel-surfing, so the expression "surfing the Web" was a natural extension of the earlier expression. But the Web is only one aspect of the internet and you label yourself as terminally uncool if you say "surfing the Internet." (Cooll people say "Net" anyway.) It makes no sense to refer to targeted, purposeful searches for information as "surfing"; for that reason I call my classes on internet research techniques "scuba-diving the Internet."

However, Jean Arm our Polly, who claims to have originated the phrase "surfing the Internet" in 1992, maintains that she intended it to have exactly the connotations it now has. See her page on the history of the term: (http://www.netmom.com/about/surfing_main.htm).

Take a different tact/take a different tack

This expression has nothing to do with tactfulness and everything to do with sailing, in which it is a direction taken as one tacks-abruptly turns-a boat. To "take a different tack" is to try another approach.

Taken Back/Taken Aback

When you're startled by something, you're taken aback by it. When you're reminded of something from your past, you're taken back to that time.

Taught/Taut

Students are taught, ropes are pulled taut.

Taunt/Taut/Tout

I am told that medical personnel often mistakenly refer to a patient's abdomen as "taunt' rather than the correct "taut—" Taunt" ("tease" or "mock") can be a verb or noun, but never an adjective. "Taut" means "tight, distended," and is always an adjective.

Don't confuse "taunt' with "tout" or which means "promote," as in "Senator Bilgewater has been touted as presidential candidate." You tout somebody you admire and taunt someone that you don't.

Tenant/Tenet

These two words come from the same Latin root, "tenure," meaning "to hold"; but they have very different meanings. "Tenet" is the rarer of the two, meaning a belief that a person holds: "Avoiding pork is a tenet of the Muslim faith." In contrast, the person leading an apartment from you is your tenant. (She holds the lease.)

Tender Hooks/Tenterhooks

A "tenter" is a canvas-stretcher, and to be "on tenterhooks" means to be as tense with anticipation as a canvas stretched on one.

Tentative

Often all-too-tentatively pronounced "tentative." Sound all three "T's."

Than/Then

When comparing one thing with another you may find that one is more appealing "than" another. "Than" is the word you want when doing comparison. But if you are talking about time, choose "then": "First you separate the eggs; then you beat the whites." Alexis is smarter than I, not "then I."

That/Which

I must confess that I do not myself observe the distinction between "that" and "which." Furthermore, there is little evidence that this distinction is or has ever been regularly made in past centuries by careful writers of English. However, a small but impassioned group of authorities has urged the distinction; so here is the information you will need to pacify them.

If you are defining something by distinguishing it from a larger class of which it is a member, use "that"; "I chose the lettuce that had the fewest wilted leaves." When the general class is not being limited or defined in some way, then "which" is appropriate: "He made an iceberg lettuce Caesar salad, which didn't taste right."

That kind/that kind of

Although expressions like "that kind thing" are common in some dialects, standard English requires "of" in this kind of phrase.

Theirselves/Themselves

There is no such word as "theirselves" (and you certainly can't spell it "theirself's" or "theirselves"); it's "themselves." And there is no correct singular form of this non-word; instead of "theirself" use "himself" or "herself."

Them/Those

One use of "them" for "those" has become standard catch phrase: "how do you like them apples?" This is deliberate dialectical humor. But "I like them little canapes with the shrimp on top" is gauche; say instead "I like those little canapes."

Therefor/Therefore

The form without a final "E" is an archaic bit of legal terminology meaning "for." The word most people want is "therefore."

There's

There's People often forget that "there's" is a contraction of "there is" and mistakenly say "there's three burrs caught in your hair" when they mean "there're" ("there are"). Use "there's only when referring to one item.

These Are Them/These Are They

Although only the pickiest listeners will cringe when you way "these are them," the traditionally correct phrase is "these are they," because "they is the predicate nominative of "these." However, if people around you seem more comfortable with "it's me" than "it's I," you might as well stick with "these are them."

These Kind/This kind

In a sentence like "I love this kind of chocolates," "this" modifies "kind" (singular) and not "chocolates" (plural), so it would be incorrect to change it to "I love these kind of chocolates." Only if "kind" itself is pluralized into "kinds" should "this" shift to "these": "You keep making these kinds of mistakes!"

These Ones/These

By itself, there's nothing wrong with the word "ones" as a plural: "surrounded by her loved ones." However, "this one" should not be pluralized to "these ones." Just say "these." The same pattern applies to "those."

They/Their (Singular)

Using the plural pronoun to refer to a single person of unspecified gender is an old and honorable pattern in English, not a newfangled bit of degeneracy or a politically correct plot to avoid sexism (though it often serves the latter purpose). People who insist that "everyone has brought his own lunch" is the only correct form do not reflect the usage of centuries of fine writers. A good general rule is that only when the singular noun does not specify an individual can it be replaced plausibly with a plural pronoun: "Everybody" is a good example. We know that "everybody" is singular because we say "everybody" is here," not "everybody are here" yet we tend to think of "everybody" as a group of individuals, so we usually say "everybody brought their own grievances to the bargaining table." "Anybody" is treated similarly.

However, in many written sentences the use of singular "their" and "they" creates an irritating clash even when it passes unnoticed in speech. It is wise to shun this popular pattern in formal writing. Often expressions can be pluralized to make the "they" or "their" indisputably proper: "All of them have brought their own lunches." "People" can often be substituted for "each." Americans seldom avail themselves of the otherwise very handy British "one" to avoid specifying gender because it sounds to our ears rather pretentious: "One's hound should retrieve only one's own grouse." If you decide to try "one," don't switch to "they" in mid-sentence: "One has to be careful about how they speak" sounds absurd because the word "one" so emphatically calls attention to its singleness. The British also quite sensibly treat collective bodies like governmental units and corporations as plural ("Parliament have approved their agenda") whereas Americans insist on treating them as singular.

They're/Their/There

Many people are so spooked by apostrophes that a word like "They're" seems to them as if it might mean almost anything. In fact, it's always a contraction of "they are." If you've written "they're," ask yourself whether you can substitute "they are." If not, you've made a mistake. "Their" is a possessive pronoun like "her" or "our": "They eat their hotdogs ith sauerkraut." Everything else is "there." "There goes the ball, out of the park! See it? Right there! There aren't very many home runs like that." "Thier is a common misspelling, but you can avoid it by remembering that "they" and "their" begin with the same three letters. Another hint: "there' has "here" buried inside it to remind you it refers to place, while "their" has "heir" buried in it to remind you that it has to do with possession.

Think on/Think About

An archaic form that persists in some dialects is seen in statements like "I'll think on it" when most people would say "I'll think about it."

Though/Thought/Through

Although most of us know the differences between these words people often type one of them when they mean another. Spelling checkers won't catch this sort of slip, so look out for it.

Throne/Thrown

A throne is that chair a king sits on, at least until he gets thrown out of office.

Thusly/Thus

"Thusly" has been around for a long time, but it is widely viewed as nonstandard. It's safer to go with plain old "thus."

Time Period

The only kinds of periods meant by people who use this phrase are periods of time, so it's a redundancy. Simply say "time" or "period."

Time smaller

Mathematically literate folds object to expressions like "my paycheck is three times smaller than it used to be" because "times" indicates multiplication and should logically apply only to increases in size. Say "one third as large" instead.

To/Too/Two

People seldom mix "two" up with the other two; it obviously belongs with words that also begin with TW, like "twice" and "twenty" that involve the number 2. But the other two are confused all the time. Just remember that the only meanings of "too" are "also" ("I want some ice cream too") and "in excess" ("Your walkman is playing too loudly.") Note that extra o. It should remind you that this word has to do with adding more on to something. "To" is the proper spelling for all the other uses.

To Home/At Home

In some dialects people say "I stayed to home to wait for the mail," but in standard English the expression is "stayed at home."

Today's Modern Society/Today

People seeking to be up-to-the-minute often indulge in such redundancies as "in today's modern society" or "in the modern society of today." This is empty arum-waving which says nothing more than "now" or "today." A reasonable substitute is "contemporary society." Such phrases are usually indulged in by people with a weak grasp of history to substitute for such more precise expressions as "for the past five years" or "this month." See "since the beginning of time."

Tolled/Told

Some people imagine that the expression should be "all tolled" as if items were being ticked of to the tolling of a bell, or involved the paying of a toll; but in fact this goes back to an old meaning of "tell": "to count." You could "tell over" your beads if you were counting them in a rosary. "All told" means "all counted."

Tongue and Cheek/Tongue in Cheek

When people want to show they are kidding or have just knowingly uttered a falsehood, they stick their tongues in their cheeks, so it's "tongue in cheek," not "tongue and cheek."

Toward/Towards

These two words are interchangeable, but "toward" is more common in the U.S. and "towards" in the U.K.

Tradegy/Tragedy

Not only do people often misspell "tragedy" as "tradegy," they mispronounce it that way too. Just remember that the adjective is "tragic" to recall that it's the G that comes after the A.

Troop/Troupe

A group of performers is a troupe. Any other group of people, military or otherwise, is a troop.

Track Home/Tract Home

Commuters from a tract home may well feel that they are engaged in a rat race, but hat does not justify them in describing their housing development as a "track." "Tract" here means an area of land on which cheap and uniform houses have been built.

Try and/Try to

Although "try and" is common in colloquial speech and will usually pass unrewarded there, in writing try to remember to use "try to" instead of "try and."

Ufo

"Ufo" stands for "Unidentified Flying Object," so if you're sure that silvery disk is an alien spacecraft, there's no point in calling it a "UFO." I love the sign in a Seattle bookstore labeling the alien-invasion section: "Incorrectly Identified Flying objects."

Unconscience/Unconscious

Do people confuse the unconscious with conscience because the stuff fermenting in one's unconscious is often stuff that bothers one's conscience? Whatever the cause, there is no such word as "unconscious." And while we're on the subject, Freudian psychology does not use "subconscious" which implies something that is merely not consciously thought of, rather than something that is suppressed, though it is used by Jungians.

Upmost/utmost

The word is "utmost," and is related to words like "utter," as in "The birthday party was utter chaos," "Upmost" may seem logical, but it's a sure sign of a person who knows spoken English better than written English.

Use to/used to

Because the D and T are blended into a single consonant when this phrase is pronounced, many writers are unaware that the D is even present and omit it in writing. See also "suppose to."

Vague Reference

Vague reference is a common problem in sentences where "this," "it," "which" or other such words don't refer back to any one specific word or phrase, but a whole situation. "I hitchhiked back to town, got picked up by an alien spacecraft and was subjected to humiliating medical experiments, which is why I didn't get my paper done on time." In conversation this sort of thing goes unnoticed, but more care needs to be taken in writing. There are lots of ways to reorganize this sentence to avoid the vague reference. You could begin the sentence with "because" and replace "which is why" with "so," for instance.

Sometimes the referent is only understood and not directly expressed at all: "Changing you oil regularly is important, which is one reason your engine burned up." The "Which' refers to an implied failure to change oil regularly, but doesn't actually refer back to any of the specific words used earlier in the sentence.

Sometimes there is no logical referent: "In the book it says that Shakespeare was in love with some "dark lady'." This is a casual way of using "it" that is not acceptable in formal written English. Write instead "Arthur O. Williams says in the sonnets that Shakespeare...."

A reference may be ambiguous because it's not clear which of two referents is meant: "Most women are attracted to guys with a good sense of humor unless they are into practical jokes." Does "they' refer to "women" or "guys"? It would be clearer if the sentence said "Most women are attracted to guys with a good sense of humor, though not usually to practical jokers."

Vary/Very

"Vary" means "to change." Don't substitute it for "very" in phrases like "very nice" or "very happy."

Veil of Tears/Vale of Tears

The expression "vale of tears" goes back to pious sentiments that consider life on earth to be a series of sorrows to be left behind when we go on to a better world in Heaven. It conjures up an image of a suffering traveler laboring through a valley ("vale") of troubles and sorrow. "Veil of tears" is poetic sounding, but it's a mistake.

Verbage/Verbiage

"Verbiage" is an insulting term usually meant to disparage needlessly wordy prose. Don't use it to mean simply "wording." There is no such word as "verbage."

Verses/Versus

The "vs." in a law case like "Brown vs. The Board of Education" stands for Latin versus (meaning "against"). Don't confuse it with the word for line of poetry—"verses"—when describing other conflicts, like the upcoming football game featuring Oakesdale versus Pinewood.

Very Unique/unique

"Unique" singles out one of a kind. That "un" at the beginning is a form of "one." A thing is unique (the only one of its kind) or it is not. Something may be almost unique (there are very few like it), but nothing is "very unique."

Vicious/Viscous circle/cycle

The term "vicious circle" was invented by logicians to describe a form of fallacious circular argument in which each term of the argument draws on the other: "Democracy is the best form of government because democratic elections produce the best governments. The phrase has been extended in popular usage to all kinds of self-exacerbating processes such as this : poor people often find themselves borrowing money to pay off their debts, but in the process create even more onerous debts which in their turn will need to be financed by further borrowing. Sensing vaguely that such destructive spirals are not closed loops, people have transmuted "vicious circle" into "vicious cycle." The problem with this perfectly logical change is that a lot of people know what the original "correct" phrase was and are likely to scorn users of the new one. They go beyond scorn to contempt however toward those poor souls who render the phrase as "viscous cycle." Don't use this expression unless you are discussing a Harley-Davidson in dire need of an oil change.

Video/film

Many of us can remember when portable transistorized radios were ignorantly called "transistors." We have a tendency to abbreviate the names of various sorts of electronic technology (see "stereo" and "satellite"), often in the process confusing the medium with the content. Video is the electronic reproduction of images, and applies to broadcast and cable television, prerecorded videocassette recordings (made on a videocassette recorder, or VCR), and related technologies. MTV appropriated this broad term for a very narrow meaning: "videotaped productions of visual material meant to accompany popular music recordings." This is now what most people mean when they speak of "a video," unless they are "renting a video," in which case they mean a Video Cassette or DVD recording of a film. One also hears people referring to theatrical films that they happened to have viewed in videotaped reproduction as "videos." This is simply wrong. A film is a film (or movie), whether it is projected on a screen from 35 to 70 mm film or broadcast via the NTSC, SECAM or PAL standard. Orson Welles" "Citizen Kane" is not now and never will be a "video."

Vinegarette/vinaigrette

Naive diners and restaurant workers alike commonly mispronounce the classic French dressing called "vinaigrette" as if it were "vinegarette." To be more sophisticated, say "vin-uh-GRETT" (the first syllable rhymes with "seen").

Vitae/Vita

Unless you are going to claim credit for accomplishments in previous incarnations, you should refer to your "vita," not your "vitae." All kidding aside, the "ae" in "vitae" supposedly indicates the genitive rather than the plural; but the derivation of "vita" from "curriculum vitae" is purely on its own makes no sense grammatically.

"Resume," by the way, is a French word with both "Es" accented, and literally means "summary." In English one often sees it without the accents, or with only the second accent, neither of which is a serious error. But if you're trying to show how multilingual you are, remember the first accent.

Viola/voila

A viola is a flower or a musical instrument. The expression which means "behold!" is "voila." It comes from a French expression literally meaning "look there!" in French it is spelled with a grave accent over the A, but when it was adopted into English, it lost its accent. Such barbarous misspellings as "vwala" are even worse, caused by the reluctance of English speakers to believe that "OI" can represent the sound "wah," as it usually does in French.

Volumptuous/voluptuous

Given the current mania for slim, taut bodies, it is understandable – if amusing – that some folks should confuse voluptuousness with lumpiness. In fact, "voluptuous" is derived from Latin "voluptas," which refers to sensual pleasure and not to shape at all. A voluptuous body is a luxurious body.

Wary/weary/lerry

People sometimes write "weary" (tired) when they mean "wary" (cautious) which is a close synonym with "leery" which in the psychedelic era was often misspelled "leary"; but since Timothy Leary faded from public consciousness, the correct spelling has prevailed.

Warrantee/warranty

Confused by the spelling of "guarantee," people often misspell the related word "warrantee" rather than the correct "warranty." "Warrantee" is a rare legal terms that means "the person to whom a warrant is made." Although "guarantee" can be a verb ("we guarantee your satisfaction"), "warranty" is not. The rarely used very form is "to warrant."

Way/far, much more

Young people frequently use phrases like "way better" to mean "far better" or "very much better." In format writing, it would be gauche to say that impressionism is "way more popular" than Cubism instead of "much more popular."

Ways/way

In some dialects it's common to say "you've got a ways to go before you've saved enough to buy a Miata," but in standard English it's "a way to do."

Weather/wether/whether

The climate is made up of "weather"; whether it is nice out depends on whether it is raining or not. A wether is just a castrated sheep.

Went/gone

The past participle of "go" is "gone" so it's not "I should have went to the party" but "I should have gone to the party."

Were/where

Sloppy typists frequently leave the "H" out of "where." Spelling checkers do not catch this sort of error, of course, so look for it as you proofread.

Wet your appetite/whet your appetite

It is natural to think that something mouth-watering "wets you appetite," but actually the expression is "whet your appetite"—sharpen your appetite, as a whetstone sharpens a knife.

What/that

In some dialects it is common to substitute "what" for "that," as in "You should dance with him what brung you." This is not standard usage.

Wheat/whole wheat

Waiters routinely ask "What or white?" when bread is ordered, but the white bread is also made of wheat. The correct term is "whole wheat," in which the whole grain, including the bran and germ, has been used to make the flour. "Whole wheat" does not necessarily imply that no white flour has been used in the bread; most whole wheat breads incorporate some white flours.

Whereabouts are/whereabouts is

Despite the deceptive "S" on the end of the word, "whereabouts" is normally singular, not plural. "The whereabouts of the stolen diamond is unknown." Only if you were simultaneously referring to two or more persons having separate whereabouts would the word be plural, and you are quite unlikely to want to do so.

Where it's at

This slang expression gained widespread currency in the sixties as a hip way of stating that the speaker understood the essential truth of a situation: "I know where it's at." Or more commonly: "You don't known where it's at." It is still heard from time to time with that meaning, but the user risks being labeled as a quaint old Boomer. However, standard usage never accepted the literal sense of the phrase. Don't say, "I put my purse down and now I don't know where it's at" unless you want to be regarded as uneducated. "Where it is" will do fine; the "at" is redundant.

Whether/whether or not

"Whether" works fine on its own in most contexts: "I wonder whether I forgot to turn off the stove?" But when you mean "regardless of whether" it has to be followed by "or not" somewhere in the sentence: "We need to leave for the airport in five minutes whether you've found your teddy bear or not."

Whilst/while

Although "whilst" is a perfectly good traditional synonym of "while," in American usage it is considered pretentious and old-fashioned.

Whim and a prayer

A 1943 hit song depicted a fighter pilot just barely managing to bring his shot-up plane back to base, "comin" in on a wing and a prayer" (lyrics by Harold Adamson, music by Jimmy McHugh). Some people who don't get the allusion mangle this expression as "a whim and a prayer." Whimsicality and fervent prayerfulness don't go together.

Whimp/wimp

The original and still by far the most common spelling of this common bit of slang meaning "weakling, coward," is "wimp." If you use the much less common "whimp" instead people may regard you as a little wimpy.

Whisky/whiskey

Scots prefer the spelling "whisky"; Americans follow instead the Irish spelling, so Kentucky bourbon is "whiskey."

Who's/whose

This is one of those cases where it is important to remember that possessive pronouns never take apostrophes, even though possessive nouns do (see it's/its). "Who" s" always and forever means only "who is," as in "Who's that guy with the droopy mustache?" or "who has," as in "Who is being eating my porridge?" "Whose" is the possessive form of "who" and is used as follows: "Whose dirty socks are these on the breakfast table?"

Who/whom

"Whom" has been dying an agonizing death for decades – you'll notice there are no Whom in Dr. Seuss's Whoville. Many people never use the word in speech at all. However, in formal writing, critical readers still expect it to be used when appropriate. The distinction between "who" and "whom" is basically simple: "who" is the subject form of this pronoun and "whom" is the object form. "Who was wearing that awful dress at the Academy Awards banquet?" is correct because "who" is the subject of the sentence. "The MC was so startled by a neckline that he forgot to whom he was supposed to give the Oscar" is correct because "whom" is the object of the preposition "to." So far so good.

Now consider this sort of question: "Who are you starting at?" Although strictly speaking the pronoun should be "whom," nobody who wants to be taken seriously would use it in this case, though it is the object of the preposition "at". (Bothered by ending the sentence with a preposition? See my "Non-Errors" section.) "Whom" is very rarely used even by carefully speakers as the first word in a question; and many authorities have now conceded the point.

There is another sort of question in which "whom" appears later in the sentence: "I wonder whom he bribed to get the contract?" This may seem at first similar to the previous example, but here "whom" is not the subject of any verb in the sentence; rather it is part of the noun clause which itself is the object of the verb "wonder." Here an old gender-biased but effective test for "whom" can be used. Try rewriting the sentence using "he" or "him." Clearly "He bribed he" is incorrect; you would say "he bribed him." Where "him" is the proper word in the paraphrased sentence, use "whom."

Instances in which the direct object appears at the beginning of a sentence are tricky because we are used to having subjects in that position and are strongly tempted to use "who" "Whomever Susan admired most was likely to get the job." (Test: "She admired him." Right?)

Where things get really messy is in statements in which the object or subject status of the pronoun is not immediately obvious. Example : "The police gave tickets to whoever had parked in front of the fire hydrant."

The object of the preposition "to" is the entire noun clause, "whoever had parked in front of the fire hydrant," but "whoever" is the subject of that clause, the subject of the very "had parked," Here's a case where the temptation to use "whoever" should be resisted.

Confused? Just try the "he or him" text, and if it's still not clear, go with "who." You'll bother fewer people and have a fair chance of being right.

A whole" Nother/ A Completely different

It is one thing to use the expression "a whole 'nother' as a consciously slangy phrase suggesting rustic charm and a completely different matter to use it mistakenly. The "A" at the beginning of the phrase is the common article "a" but is here treated as if it were simultaneously the first letter of "another," interrupted by "whole."

-wise

In political and business jargon it is common to append "-wise" to nouns to create novel adverbs: "Revenue-wise, last quarter was a disaster." Critics of language are united in objecting to this pattern, and it is often used in fiction to satirize less than eloquent speakers.

Woman/women

The singular "woman" probably gets mixed up the plural "women" because although both are spelled with an O in the first syllable, only the pronunciation of the O really differentiates them. Just remember that this word is treated no differently than "man" (one person) and "men" (more than one person). A woman—never a women.

World wide web

"World Wide Web" is a name that needs to be capitalized, like "Internet." It is made up of Web pages and Web sites (or, less formally, Websites).

Worse comes to Worse/worst comes to worst

That traditional idiom is "if worst comes to worst." The modern variation "worse comes to worst" is a little more logical. "Worse comes to worse" is just a mistake.

Would have liked to have/would have liked

"She would liked to have had another glass of champagne" should be "she would have liked to have another glass..."

Wreckless/reckless

This word has nothing to do with creating the potential for a wreck. Rather it involves not reckoning carefully all the hazards involved in an action. The correct spelling is therefore "reckless."

Writing/writing

One of the comments English teachers dread to see on their evaluation is "The professor really helped me improve my writing. "When "-ing" is added to a word which ends in a short vowel followed only by a single consonant, the consonant is normally doubled, but "write" has a silent E on the end to ensure the long I sound in the word. Doubling the T in this case would make the word rhyme with "flitting."

Ya'll/y'all

"How y' all doin" ?" if you are rendering this common Southernism in print, be careful where you place the apostrophe, which stands for the second and third letters in "you." "Y'all" is properly used only when addressing two or more people.

Ye/the

Thos. who study the history of English know that the word often misr.ad as "ye" in Middle English is good old "the" spelled with an unfamiliar character called a "thorn" which looks vaguely like a "Y" but which is pronounced "TH." So all those quaint shop names beginning "Ye Olde" are based on a confusion: people never said "Ye" to mean "the." However, if you'd rather be cute than historically accurate, go ahead. Very few people will know any better.

Yea/yeah/yay

"Yea" is a very old-fashioned formal way of saying "yes," used mainly in voting. It's the opposite of—and rhymes with—"nay." When you want to write the common casual version of "yes," the correct spelling is "yeah" (sound like "yeh"). When the third grade teacher announced a class trip to the zoo, we all yelled "yay!" (the opposite of "boo"!). that was back when I was only yay big.

Yoke/yolk

The yellow center of an egg is its yolk. The link that holds two oxen together is a yoke; they are yoked.

Your/You

"I appreciate you cleaning the toilet" is more formal than "I appreciate you cleaning the toilet."

Your/You're

"You're" is always a contraction of "you are." If you've written "you're," try substituting "you are." If it doesn't work, the word you want is "your." Your writing will improve if you're careful about this.

You've Got Another Thing Coming/You've Got Another Think Coming

Here's a case in which eagerness to avoid error leads to error. The original expression is the last part of a deliberately ungrammatical joke: "if that's what you think, you've got another think coming."

CHAPTER 7

Summary of Common Errors

The Comma Splice

The comma splice is the incorrect joining of two independent clauses with a comma is an extremely common error. Most frequently students connect two short sentences:

They believe in Oedipus, he is their king.

There are three ways to solve this problem:

1. Use a period to separate the clauses into two sentences:

   They believe in Oedipus. He is their king.

2. Join the clauses with a coordinating or subordinating conjunction, depending on their relation to one another.

   They believe on Oedipus, for he is their king.

3. Join the clauses with a semicolon:

   They believe in Oedipus; he is their king.

In this particular example, using the first option would result in sentences that are too short, too choppy. There is an obvious connection between the clauses which is best expressed through a conjunction; therefore, the second option is the best to use here.

In the following example, however, the writer has used a comma where a semi-colon is appropriate.

Sgnarelle is not the primary character, still he acts as a foil.

The clauses could form separate sentences, but the use of "still" implies a stronger link which is best served by a semi-colon:

Sgnarelle is not the primary character; still, he acts as a foil.

In this example, the clauses being connected are too complex to be part of the same sentences:

> Lear was a majestic ruler when he was young, however, as he became older, his temptations clouded his thought.

> Lear was a majestic ruler when he was young, However, as he became older, his temptations clouded his thought.

The writer could use a conjunction:

> Lear was a majestic ruler when he was young, but as he became older his temptations clouded his thought.

A comma cannot, by itself, connect two main clauses; the clauses must either form separate sentences or be joined by a coordinating conjunction. For main clauses, see the Short Treatise on Grammar and the "tip" after "sentence fragments" in this section.

Note that *conjunctive adverbs* have the logical effect of linking ideas, but do not link sentences grammatically. In the last example the world however is none of these. Others to watch for are *therefore*, *thus*, and *this*.

Run-on Sentences

A run-on sentence fuses two sentences together without any punctuation:

They believe in Oedipus he is their king.

This problem can be fixed in the same three ways as the *comma splice.*

FRAGMENTS

A sentence fragment is a piece o a sentence which has been punctuated as if it were a complete sentence. Usually it is a phrase or subordinate clause which has been improperly separated from a main clause.

> Matt has been improving at shcool. *Since he stopped skipping class.*
>
> It was the time of year when the neighbours would suddenly become uncharacteristically generous, pressing quantities of enormous zucchini on us. *It being the most prolific or vegetables.*

The sentences must be reconnected:

> *Matt has been improving at school since he stopped skipping class.*
>
> *It was the time of year when the neighbours would suddenly become uncharacteristically generous, pressing quantities of enormous zucchini on us, it being the most prolific of vegetables.*

Every sentence must have a main clause, and thus a complete verb.

Particularly in works of fiction, a sentence fragment can be a rhetorically effective device, but in formal writing it is more likely to be simply inept.

A tip: if you are unsure of the distinction between a complete verb and an incomplete one, or a main clause and a *participle* phrase, there is a simple test you can apply to find out if you have a sentence fragment, or a comma splice:

- Each complete sentence will make a complete statement, and each complete statement must be either true or false.
- Thus if you ask of the fragment above – "Since he stopped skipping class": true or false—there can be no

answer (what happened since he stopped?). and thus it is not a complete sentence.

- Similarly, both parts of the comma splice can be tested ("They believed in Oedipus" and "He is their king"– both can be answered, in this case as "true"), so there are two complete statements.

WORDINESS

As wordiness is the writer's bane, we have covered it from various angles throughout this manual. Always dump the excess baggage from your essay; it will fly higher as a result.

- Avoid overusing relative pronouns such as *which* and *that.* Often they can be eliminated. For example, "The dog that you found yesterday" can be shortened to "The dog you found yesterday." The link is obvious.

- Avoid overusing *meaningless qualifiers* such as *quite, extremely* and *very*. Words such as these have lost their potency through overuse, and have become filler. Use a stronger word instead (*exhausted* rather than *very tired*). Many of these qualifiers appear in the Usage dictionary. Also stay away from phrases like "A great many of ..." and "A great deal of..."

- Avoid *ponderous* or *vague construction* such as *despite the fact that, due to the fact that, an aspect of, and the use of.*

- Avoid excessively *tentative language* such as *it seems that* and *appears to suggest*. Not only is it wordy, it also makes your argument appear weak. Only use these contractions if there is genuine uncertainty. If you are at all confident, writes as if you are.

- Avoid *redundancies*. Do not write that someone is *naive* and *innocent* or *dull and boring*. These words are virtual synonyms. You do not have to provide a list where a single world will do. Be aware of a word's implications; for example, if you tell the reader that a woman is wearing a hat, you do not need to add "on her head." The reader will assume that hat is on her head because it is the nature of hats to be found on heads (if she is wearing it elsewhere, then it is worth mentioning).

- Avoid the *passive vice* which is possibly the greatest cause of wordiness.

THE PASSIVE VOICE

In most cases, avoid the passive voice ("Jim is being driven to distraction by his hamster") in favor of the more concise active voice ("Jim hamster is driving him to distraction"). A sentence is more effective when it centers on a subject that is doing something, rather than a subject that is being acted upon.

The passive voice is useful under certain circumstances; for example, if the precise subject of the action is not known ("My car was spray-painted last night") or if the receiver of the action is more important ("The Emperor was assassinated last night"). However, more often than not passive sentences can be improved by reworking the sentence so that the very is active.

The main problem with passive sentences is that they are wordy: "The theme that was most dealth with by the 16th Century poets was ..." can easily be condensed into "The 16th Century poets most often dealt with the theme of ..." This next sentence is virtually incomprehensible because it uses too many passive" Another illustration of the word 'master' being used to define material things as being the controlling element is ..."

When you are providing examples, avoid passive constructions such as:

- "This is also seen when..."
- "It can be seen that ..."
- "It is shown that..."

and so on. If you find it necessary to introduce material in this way, use active verbs: "One [we, I] can see that..."

Writers often use the passive voice to avoid "I", because they have been told from an early age that "I" is unacceptable. Different academic disciplines, and different instructors within those disciplines, have varying attitudes the use of the personal pronoun: you would be wise to check. However, the sparing use of "I" can be an alternative to unwieldy passives like some of those cited above: "I think..." is both more effective stylistically and more honest than "It is thought that ..." The passive is often used to avoid responsibility: "The economy of this Province has been mismanaged" is less incriminating than "We have mismanaged the economy of this Province."

Do not shift from active to passive in the same sentence:

> As I entered the mansion, footsteps could be heard from behind me.

Both the verb and subject have shifted. The sentence should read:

> As I entered the mansion, I heard footsteps behind me.

Parallelism

The ability to write a good parallel sentence is invaluable in easy work. Faulty parallelism, on the other hand, produces an effect in your reader similar to changing gears without using the clutch. A successful parallel sentence reads smoothly, while a faulty parallel sentence lurches awkwardly.

The previous sentence is an example of good parallelism because it obeys the technique's central rule: The grammatical elements of parallel clauses must match. The following sentence is an example of poor parallelism because the vary form changes:

> This debate begun in Greece and which continues into modern times.
>
> Begun is a participial adjective while continues is an active verb. The sentence should read:
>
> This debate began in Greece and continues into modern times.

The rule applies not only to verbs but also to nouns, adjectives, adverbs and other parts of speech. In the following sentence, for example, a noun has been mixed with a pair of verbal nouns (gerunds):

> I acquired my considerable fortune by investing carefully, hard work and marrying a rich woman.

The sentence should read:

> I acquired my considerable fortune by investing carefully, working hard and marrying a rich woman.

Watch for grammatical signposts that point to the need for careful parallel constructions.

- Linking words (such as and, or yet and but) often indicators of the need for parallel structure:

  "I lost my heart in San Francisco, but I left my shoes in Santa Fe."

  Parallel constructions also follow

  as

  is better to give than to appear cheap. Here, the to must be repeated to preserve the infinitive structure.

- Correlative conjunctions (pairs such as either ... or and both... and) introduce clauses that must be parallel. The following sentence is incorrect because the very forms are mixed.

  "We can either drive to the Grand Canyon or we're flying to Japan."

  The indecisive vacationer should say

  "We can either drive to the Grand Canyon or fly to Japan."

  Not only... but also can be tricky because of the placement of only and also, but the same rules apply.

"He is not only the nicest person I have ever met, but also the most fragrant man I have ever sniffed."

In a not... neither construction, the first negation can affect the meaning of the second. For example, if you write

"Justin is not an ordinary person, and neither are his stories,"

you are implying that the stories are not ordinary people. A more accurate assessment of Justin would be,

"Justin is not an ordinary, and neither are his stories,"

- Lists also need to be parallel:

"I like a good lunch, singing and to read:

should read

"I like eating a good lunch, singing and reading."

Parallelism is especially effective for thesis sentences, because you can incorporate all the sections of your argument in a unified manner:

"Because they are dangerous for children, they stick to carpets, and they are expensive to produce, Slime Balls should be banned from toy stores."

The parallel structure provides a clarity and balance which sharpens your thesis; in this instance the parallels also point the way to the three paragraphs you will be writing to support the thesis.

SUBJECT/VERB AGREEMENT

Be sure that your subject agrees with the very, even when there are intervening components of the sentence. In the sentence,

The group of bizarrely dressed youths are taking over the cafeteria.

The writer has used a plural verb because of the proximity of youths, but the subject of the sentence is group. The sentence should read:

> The group of bizarrely dressed youths is taking over the cafeteria.

If there are two subjects joined by and, use a plural verb:

> My mother and father are coming to visit.

If the subjects are joined by or, the verb must agree with the nearest subject:

> Either Danny or Sandy is handling it.

> Either Sherlock Holmes or the Hardy Boys are capable of solving this crime.

Collective nouns such as family take singular verbs when the sentence deals with the group as a whole:

> The Griswold family is going on vacation this year.

If the sentence deals with the family as individuals, then a plural form is used:

> The Griswold family are going to fight all the way through their vacation.

Linking verbs in subjective completions agree with the subject, not the completion:

> My favourite thing to buy is compact discs.

But compare:

> Compact discs are my favourite thing to buy.

PRONOUN AGREEMENT

Pronouns agree in gender and number. This rule is not difficult to remember if you are writing about individual people or inanimate objects (where it suffices for everything). However, collective pronouns present more of a problem. Indefinite words such as anyone, anything, someone, everybody and no one take singular pronouns. Pronouns are also an issue when using gender-specific language.

The antecedent is the noun to which the pronoun refers. Make sure that it is clear what the antecedent of a pronoun is; otherwise, confusion and ambiguity will prevail. Also, make sure that you are referring to the correct noun. For example, in the following sentence the pronoun their refers to the noun people and not to one:

> You are one of those people who like to keep their skeletons in the closet.

In this next sentence, however, the pronoun his refers to one and not to members:

> I am the only one of the Lodge members who never wears his fez.

Be aware of the case of the pronoun. (For a discussion of case, see the section on grammar, 1.5.) If it is acting as the subject of a verb, use the subjective form:

> It was she.

She is the subjective completion of "it was". Many people would automatically write "It was her," but the verb to be takes the same case after as before.

If the pronoun is acting as an object, use the objective form, even if the first person is involved:

> Josh was angry with him and me.

Many writers believe it is improper to write "him and me," but this is only true in the subjective case. It is not correct to write this:

> Ken and me went to the ballgame,

But it is also incorrect to write

The rain soaked Ken and I,

or

They sent the invitation to Ken and I.

Use I in the subjective case and me in the objective case, no matter what other pronouns are found in the sentence. More information is available in the discussion of agreement as a grammatical issue.

The need for sentence variation

It is difficult to read an essay made up entirely of simple subject-verb sentences: "The dog is barking. Jim kicks the dog. The dog bites Jim, "While short sentences can be effective for emphasis ("The Eagle has landed"), they need to be surrounded by different kinds of sentences for contrast.

Simple sentences are the main stylistic feature of children's reader like Fun with Dick and Jane, so a paper full of them will sound as if it was written for youngster. If your essay has any claim to sophistication whatsoever, it will feature sentences of varied length and complexity.

If you find that your essay is composed of choppy little sentences, try to connect some of them into compound or complex sentences.

Misplaced modifiers

A modifying word or phrase should be placed next to the word it describes. In the following sentence, the modifying phrase has been misplaced:

Growing at the bottom of the glass, Alison found some mold.

Since it is the mold that is growing at the bottom of the glass, rather than Alison, the sentence should read:

Alison found some mold growing at the bottom of the glass.

DANGLING MODIFIER

A dangling modifier modifies a word which has been left out of the sentence:

"After writing all that material, the computer didn't save it."

The computer did not do the writing, what is actually meant is "After writing that material, I discovered that the computer didn't save it," (or, more honestly, "After writing all that material, I forgot to save it"). The subject I was omitted from the original sentence.

The positioning of limiting modifiers such as only, nearly and almost is especially important. "Only Frank dropped the bomb," "Frank only dropped the bomb" and "Frank dropped the only bomb" all have different meanings.

SQUINTING MODIFIER

A squinting modifier appears in the middle of the sentence, where its object is not clear: "I said eventually I would do it." The writer could mean

"Eventually, I said I would do it"

or

"I said would do it eventually."

MIXED METAPHORS

A mixed metaphor attempts to create an extended comparison but fails because it is not consistent with itself. For example, in an essay on the language used in describing pain relief medicine, a student wrote:

> "The topic of pain relievers seems clouded in a sea of medical terminology."

The metaphor is mixed because the images of cloud and sea do not match. The student should have said either "drowned in the sea of medical terminology" or "clouded in a fog of medical terminology." Metaphor can be effective, but do not put too much weight on your own ingenuity; it might collapse under the strain.

Notes

Notes